INSCRIPTION

Published in association with the
Royal Institute of British Architects
Drawings Collection

Margaret Richardson

Architects of the Arts and Crafts Movement

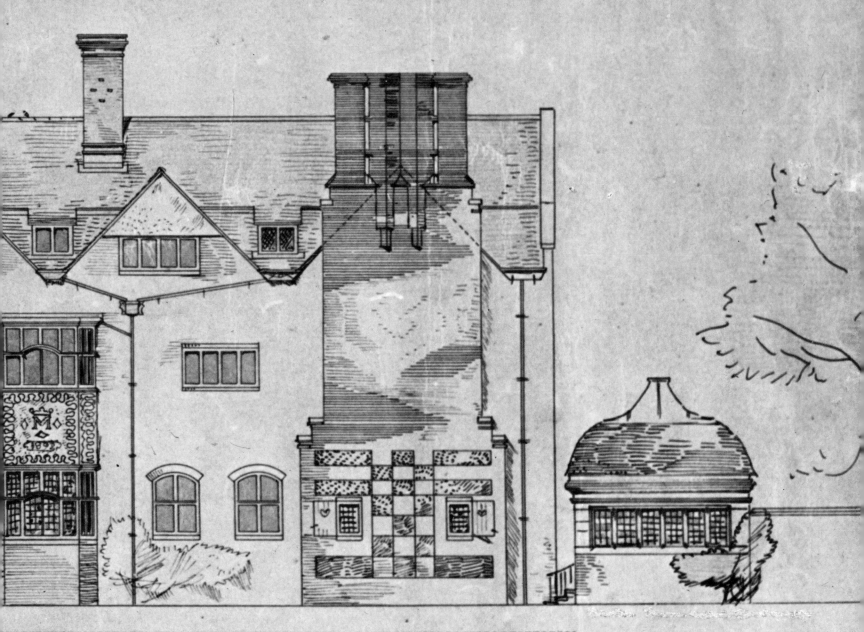

Trefoil Books, London

Title page: William Richard Lethaby, design for Avon Tyrrell for Lord Manners, 1981. Pen, blue wash and red crayon (425 x 725).

Half title: Francis Donkin Bedford (1864-1954). Design for a frame for a mirror in carved and inlaid woods, made for the Quarto Imperial Club, II, p. 50, 1895. Sepia pen, watercolour and pencil (360 x 255).

Published by
Trefoil Books Ltd.,
7 Royal Parade,
Dawes Road,
London SW6

The publishers wish to acknowledge the generous
support of the Headley Trust in the preparation
and production of this book.

ISBN 0 86294 032 X (paperback)
ISBN 0 86294 031 1 (cloth)

Set in Baskerville by Elephant Productions
and printed and bound by The Pitman Press, Bath and
E.T. Heron Ltd., Witham.

Contents

The colour plates are on pages 33-44 and 81-93.

Foreword

Acknowledgements

The Royal Institute of British Architects is very proud to be the custodian of its incomparable British Architectural Library, of which the Drawings Collection forms an important part. In scope the Collection is the largest and most comprehensive body of architectural designs in the world, with a quarter of a million drawings from the Renaissance to the present day. It is naturally orientated towards British drawings, great numbers of them presented by the architects themselves, but it also contains some magnificent continental groups, notably the Drummond Stewart collection of baroque theatre designs and the Burlington Devonshire collection which includes almost all the surviving drawings of Palladio, perhaps the most influential architect in history.

The Collection is exhaustively organised, but the use made of it by the whole international community imposes very considerable pressures on the RIBA, for published catalogues are of necessity costly. I was delighted, therefore, when the Headley Trust asked us to find a way to produce a number of illustrated books to make the treasures of the Collection known to a wider public, and to follow this by travelling exhibitions on some of the themes selected.

The fruit of this enlightened patronage is the present series of substantially illustrated books, each supported by a scholarly text, on widely different aspects of the Collection. I am confident that they will give as much pleasure to others as they have given me.

Owen Luder
President, Royal Institute of British Architects

I doubt if the die-hards of the Arts and Crafts Movement would have liked this book, as they did not care for 'pretty' pictures — nor did they like the RIBA. I have tried, therefore, to include as many design drawings as possible and to describe building materials with the names of the craftsmen and contractors, where these are known.

It may seem strange that, in a book on this subject, there are no drawings included by A.H. Mackmurdo, Charles Rennie Mackintosh or M.H. Baillie Scott. This is because the RIBA Drawings Collection has no Mackmurdo drawings and only rather poor examples by Mackintosh and Baillie Scott. Their work has, however, been exhaustively covered in the last twenty years, and their absence has allowed space to be found for some of the un-sung heroes of the Movement — good, solid, working architects like Walter Cave and Charles Spooner, Sydney Castle and A.J. Penty. It is far sadder that we have nothing in the Collection to represent the work of R.A. Briggs, E. Guy Dawber, James MacLaren, Arnold B. Mitchell, George Sherrin and F.W. Troup. I hope we will acquire examples of their work one day.

It would have been very difficult to compile this picture book without the indispensable books on the period by Peter Davey and Alastair Service, and I am grateful to them both. I would also like to thank the following for their help and advice: Jill Allibone, Nicholas Antram, Colin Baylis, John Brandon-Jones, Geremy Butler (who took the photographs), Bruce Castle, Alan Crawford, David Dean, Mary Greensted, John Harris, Jill Lever, Stephen Levrant, Mervyn Miller, Karen Moon, David Ottewill, Jane Preger, Andrew Saint, Gavin Stamp, John F. Smith, Lynne Walker, and Anthony Richardson (for telling me about buildings).

Margaret Richardson

Introduction

Baudelaire, reviewing the 1855 International Exhibition in Paris, tried to define the national characteristics of the British section. He found exotic colour, fantasy and theatrical gesture, but also its 'intimate glimpses of home'. In the 1850s and 1860s the impulse to paint genre and domestic scenes reached its peak, some having a radical purpose which was not always considered appropriate for a fine art.

Fifty years later, in 1904-1905, in his *Das Englische Haus*, Hermann Muthesius set out to characterise the 'exemplary qualities of the English house'. It is a splendid picture: the Englishman 'building for himself alone', 'self-sufficient and feeling no great urge for sociability, pursuing his own interests in virtual isolation', 'hurrying up to town for the sole purpose of doing his business' and 'hastening back to the heart of his family' in rural isolation in natural surroundings. But Muthesius pointed out that the down-to-earth qualities he so admired were not based on a 'style' but on simple vernacular buildings. The vernacular, like genre painting, was not at first considered an appropriate manner for architecture.

The vernacular became the chief preoccupation of the architects working in the 1880s and 1890s, who tried to free their work from historical styles. Most of them joined the new progressive societies and guilds and their architecture came to be called 'Arts and Crafts', after the name given to the Arts and Crafts Exhibition Society in 1888. Their drawings form the subject of this book.

The work of these architects had certain common features. Plans and elevations became the expression of utility; a building's materials were taken from its locality, being cheaper and in harmony with its surroundings. Details were based on vernacular originals and not taken from classical pattern-books. All the architects were interested in craft and in employing plasterers, painters, carvers and sculptors to enrich a building. Ornament was based on nature.

With the Arts and Crafts Movement, as David Watkin has said, went a strong love for England and things English,[1] and hence a return to English garden design of before the mid eighteenth century and a liking for artisan seventeenth century classicism as well as the vernacular. Gertrude Jekyll's definition of vernacular was 'The local tradition in building is the crystallisation of local need, material and ingenuity. When the result is so perfect, that is to say, when the adaptation of means to ends is so satisfactory that it has held good for a long time, and that no local need or influence can change it for the better; it becomes a style, and remains fixed until other conditions arise to disturb it.'[2] These words well express the dedication the Arts and Crafts architects had to local traditional building.

Although these features were common to the Movement, there were as well many variations and inconsistencies in theory and in ways of building. There were those who concentrated on the 'essentials', like C.F.A. Voysey, E.S. Prior and W.R. Lethaby; others were more interested in elaborate craft than building, for instance Gerald Horsley. There were the church architects like Sedding, Temple Moore and Comper who chose to develop a modern crafted Gothic based not on French prototypes but on English Perpendicular, and those who turned to Byzantine models for anti-Gothic reasons, such as Pite, Bentley and Sydney Barnsley. Some, like Halsey Ricardo, wanted colourful washable surfaces to buildings and different again were those who based their work on late seventeenth century vernacular styles, for example Ernest Newton. There was also the 'artiness' of Baillie Scott, and the romantic vernacular of Lutyens, both of whom had many imitators.

It must have been a hectic, exciting time throughout the 1880s and 1890s for a craft architect. Reginald Blomfield remembers that 'it was characteristic of those meetings that we talked a great deal but came to no agreement.'[3] An architect trained at that time in an office where the pupil's parent paid for his son to be articled for a set period. Articled pupils could also attend lessons in the evenings, usually from 6-9 pm, three evenings a week; at the South Kensington Schools, Royal Academy Schools or at the Architectural Association. There would have been cross-currents of ideas; the individuality of specific office methods contrasted with theoretical teaching. It was the era of guilds and societies. The first was the Society for the Protection of Ancient Buildings, SPAB, founded by

William Morris in 1877 'to keep a watch on old monuments, to protect against all "restoration" that means more than keeping out wind and weather, and, by all means, literary and other, to awaken a feeling that our ancient buildings are not mere ecclesiastical toys, but sacred monuments of the nation's growth and hope.'[4] The architect members in the first year were few — just J.F. Bentley, E.R. Robson, J.J. Stevenson, Philip Webb and George Aitchison. Painters, art patrons and men in public life were far more numerous and included Millais, Rossetti, Holman Hunt, Coventry Patmore, Sir Charles Dilke, Sir John Lubbock, Eustace Balfour and the Baroness Burdett Coutts — a list which gives some idea of how Morris was regarded in his time. But SPAB did have, of all the guilds and societies, the most important effect on architecture. For it made the younger architects of the 1880s and 1890s aware of the materials and textures of building and the value of old skills and craftsmanship. SPAB's nickname, 'Anti-scrape', carried with it the reaction to machine-made, machine-cut Minton tiles and stone used by the restorers. It was the reaction of younger architects to the hard brick and elaboration of the Gothic Revival and the terracotta eclecticism of contemporary civic architecture. There are paradoxes, however, for Alfred Waterhouse, largely a commercial architect, was an early SPAB member, whereas Nesfield and Shaw did not belong, as they both did church restorations! SPAB gave Morris countless platforms to lecture from on conservation and the right way of building, where he drew attention to such buildings as the Great Coxwell Barn, Gloucestershire — 'unapproachable in its dignity, as beautiful as a cathedral, yet with no ostentation of the builder's art',[5] believing that barns, together with cottages, should be prototypes for future building — and so they became (Lethaby's Brockhampton Church and A. Randall Wells's Kempley Church are both derived from the structure of a barn). Lorimer, lecturing on Morris in Edinburgh in 1897, said that Morris had pursued the 'spirit' of Gothic, not the letter: it was quite impossible to restore an old Gothic building — only to 'mend' it.[6]

But probably even more important than Morris's influence was the accessibility SPAB gave its members to Philip Webb. Webb had a very small office with one or two assistants and did not publish his work but was consistently the most respected and imitated architect of the Movement. He attended the SPAB meetings and the famous suppers at Gatti's restaurant afterwards. Charles Winmill who became Secretary of SPAB in 1898 recalls a typical evening: 'It all came back to me — the "after-meetings" of Anti-Scrape when we went over to Gatti's. Lethaby, who generally had a cruet of red wine with his food, Webb a half-bottle of Graves. Emery Walker, who seemed to eat the whole fish, skin, bones, and all. I think it was Sydney Cockerell who now and again had his chocolate made with milk instead of water.'[7] Lethaby, Ernest

Gimson and Sydney and Edward Barnsley were all SPAB members undertaking restoration work for the Society.

Another stimulating meeting ground was the Art Workers' Guild. This was founded in 1884 by five pupils from R.N. Shaw's office: Gerald Horsley, W.R. Lethaby, Ernest Newton, Mervyn Macartney and Edward Prior and their aims were to bring together craftsmen in architecture, painting, sculpture and the kindred arts in a practical working association where their respective theories and skills could be exchanged. The reasons for such an association were several at the time. The Royal Academy was 'now giving its favour almost entirely to oil painting' and did not exhibit crafts at all. The RIBA, it was felt, 'had opened its doors so widely to business that Surveyors had become the largest element of its body'. This criticism reflected the bitter discussion in the 1880s and 1890s as to whether architecture should, as the RIBA hoped, be put on a professional footing with a central professional body setting educational standards, or whether it ought to remain essentially a craft taught by masters to apprentices. Naturally the Art Workers' Guild's members sided with the arts and crafts, and later, in 1892, gave expression to their views in a book edited by Shaw and Jackson, *Architecture, a Profession or an Art?*

The Guild's membership is interesting. In its first decade up to 1894, 65 of its 250 members were architects, and its five influential founder members were all architects, but very few architectural subjects were discussed at its meetings. In its first two years there was only one architectural subject — 'Architecture, from the different craftsmen's points of view'. It was the architects who wanted contact with the crafts rather than vice versa.

In 1888 another Society was founded principally to exhibit the craft work of the members of the Guild, which had chosen not to open its doors to the public. It came to be called the Arts and Crafts Exhibition Society (the term 'Arts and Crafts' being originated by the bookbinder T. J. Cobden-Sanderson) and held its first exhibition at the New Gallery in Regent Street in 1888. The Society enabled the architect members of both associations to exhibit their pieces — for example Lethaby, Blomfield, Macartney, Gimson and Sydney Barnsley, acting as designers rather than craftsmen, had set up a furniture company in 1890 called Kenton & Co. The Royal Academy's Annual Exhibition in May, however, was still the leading exhibition for architectural drawings and received exhaustive reviews in the *Builder* from May-July each year. The establishment and the avant-garde alike contributed to it.

There were other progressive guilds. The Century Guild was founded by Arthur Heygate Mackmurdo in 1882 'to render all branches of art the sphere no longer of the tradesman but of the artist.' It was a commercial venture, principally making metalwork and furniture, and produced the *Hobby Horse* in 1884, a magazine devoted to a revival of arts and crafts. In 1888 C.R. Ashbee started the Guild of Handicraft, again a commercial venture, designing woodwork, metalwork, silverware and jewellery.

Guilds such as these, however, can have made very little impact on a young architect in comparison with the evening classes already mentioned and the rapidly expanding architectural press. Until the early 1890s the three most influential periodicals were the *Builder,* the *Building News,* and the more avant-garde *British Architect.* E.W. Godwin and J.D. Sedding wrote regularly in the latter in the early years of the 1880s and did much to encourage the vernacular and handicraft. The *Building News* and the *British Architect* both ran designing clubs, setting regular competitions, publishing and judging the entrants in great detail. Then came four extremely influential new magazines: *Academy Architecture*, started in 1889, which published most of the designs exhibited at the annual Academy Show; the *Studio*, very much a protagonist of the Arts and Crafts Movement, begun in 1893; the *Architectural Review* in 1896, and *Country Life* in 1897.

Finally, beset by all these progressive ideals, stimulated by much fervent talk about originality and freedom and the 'House Beautiful', the young architect spent his weekends and holidays on 'scrambles', touring Sussex, Kent, Gloucestershire and Shropshire, sketching and measuring and looking for ideas.

One wonders what the strongest influence was on a young architect of the 1880s and 1890s. No matter how many fervent meetings he attended, one suspects it was the office where he learnt to trace, to go on site, to detail and to draw.

Abbreviations in the text:

SPAB — Society for the Protection of Ancient Buildings ('Anti-Scrape')
RIBA — Royal Institute of British Architects
LCC — London County Council
AA — Architectural Association
RA — Royal Academy
PRA — President of the Royal Academy
BNDC — Building News Designing Club
FS — Full size
c. — circa

Notes on the illustrations

Measurements are given in millimetres, height before width. Dates are given only the first time the architect is mentioned.

Notes

1. David Watkin *The Rise of Architectural History*, 1980, Chapter IV.
2. Gertrude Jekyll *Old West Surrey*, 1904, pp. 5-6.
3. Reginald Blomfield *Memoirs of an Architect*, 1932, p. 70 (speaking of congresses of the National Association for the Advancement of Art and its Application to Industry and other progressive meetings).
4. Letter to the Athenaeum, 5 March 1877 quoted in J.W. Mackail *The Life of William Morris*, 1899, Vol. 1, pp. 341-2.
5. Peter Davey *Architecture of the Arts and Crafts Movement*, 1980, p. 25.
6. *Peter Savage Lorimer and the Edinburgh Craft Designers*, 1980, p. 65.
7. *Charles Canning Winmill. An Architect's Life*, by his daughter, 1946, p. 28.

Bidborough . Kent .

August 4th/62

1 Richard Norman Shaw (1831-1912). Sketch of
a brick and tile-hung cottage at Bidborough,
Kent, 4 August 1862, Shaw Sketchbook II,
p. 186. Pencil (205 x 130).

On the same day and in the same sketchbook,
Shaw sketched a tile-hung cottage at Tunbridge
Wells; Devey's Leicester Square cottages at
Penshurst; Penshurst Place, and iron door
furniture at Bidborough.

Precursors and Masters

George Devey (1820-1886) was one of the first Victorian architects to design new buildings based on the local vernacular. He had a large 'country house' practice but his earliest known work is his design for cottages at Penshurst (1850), in Kent (Colour plate I). Cottage buildings had previously been designed to classical or Gothic Revival models, or, like Nash, as picturesque *cottages ornées.* Devey, however, had an unusual and wide knowledge of country craftsmanship, related both to buildings, and to harnesses, whips, carriages and coaches. It is likely that he acquired his interest in designing vernacular buildings as a result of his training under John Sell Cotman. Devey studied under Cotman at Norwich for two years, probably from 1836-1838, and the training at that time consisted largely in making replica copies of the master's drawings, often pricking them through.

Cotman's studies at that time were often of tumbledown cottages[1] and they provide prototypes for the buildings Devey was later to design. That Devey's interest, in the Penshurst design, was not merely picturesque is clear from the mixed use of local materials prescribed on the drawing: 'Rough cast, weather boarding', and the instruction 'The workmanship etc of this front in no respect different from any other part'. He also built the Leicester Square cottages at Penshurst, shops, estate buildings, a rustic well and a barn, dated 1850, the design for which is in the RIBA Drawings Collection. All Devey's designs for estate cottages, lodges and stables are in a vernacular style.

He did not, however, wish to apply the vernacular to his designs for large country houses and these are in a mixture of styles to give the impression of gradual growth over several centuries. Devey did not publish his designs, but Salvin, Shaw and Nesfield were all aware of his work and visited Penshurst. The Architectural Association visited the village in 1886. C.F.A. Voysey became one of Devey's assistants in 1880-1882, and his early work is based on his master's vernacular manner.

Richard Norman Shaw (1831-1912) and William Eden Nesfield (1835-1888), old friends, and later partners from 1866-1869, first sketched vernacular buildings on a tour of Yorkshire in the summer of 1861. In 1862 Shaw was again sketching, this time in Kent (Fig. 1) and looking at Devey's cottages at Penshurst. In September 1862 Nesfield and Shaw joined up for a sketching tour through Sussex, filling their sketchbooks (both in the RIBA) with vernacular subjects: tile-hung, hipped-roofed cottages and shops, church furniture, architectural details: sketchbooks that were to provide models for the next thirty years.

Very soon afterwards Nesfield and Shaw's 'Old English' style emerges. Nesfield's work for Lord Crewe on the Crewe Hall Estate, Cheshire, 1864-1867, was all in this new style (Fig. 2), derived from their tour of Sussex in 1862. Nesfield's Regent's Park Lodge of 1864, his first essay in the manner, had introduced Wealden vernacular to London — a prototype easily seen by the architectural world.

Shaw's bird's eye perspective of Leyswood, near Groombridge in Sussex, dated March 1868, (Fig. 3) was exhibited at the Royal Academy in 1870 and was his first work there. It was radically different from the standard country house of the 1860s, being in the 'Old English' style, and instead of a single monumental block was designed as a cluster of different elements and roofs of varying heights around a courtyard. Merrist Wood (Figs. 4, 5), designed ten years later than Leyswood, is a further example of Shaw's 'Old English' style but conceived on a

2 William Eden Nesfield (1835-1888). Design for a detached cottage in Weston Village on the Crewe Hall Estate, Cheshire, 1865. Pen and coloured washes (365 x 655).

The cottage is built of brick, tile-hung, with hipped gables, tile cresting and incised ornament (here the Japanese sunflower motif). Nesfield's work for Lord Crewe included Stowford Cottages, Smithy Cottage (now altered), Weston Lodge, Fir Tree and a farmhouse, all datable to 1864-1867 and in the 'Old English' style.

3 Richard Norman Shaw. Bird's-eye perspective of Leyswood, near Groombridge, Sussex, for James William Temple. Pen (575 x 840).

The 'Old English' of Leyswood was radically different from the standard Gothic country house of the 1860s. The impression given is of Tudor half-timbered fragments and towers, with great seventeenth century chimneys, linked by rustic vernacular ranges. Muthesius could see the design's dependence on vernacular building styles, but it is interesting to see that the *Builder* disapproved of this particular element, saying that it was a 'revival of the past which it is more lawful to indulge in a private house for the gratifying of a man's own taste, than in more public places.' (*Builder,* XXVIII, 1870, p. 359). Shaw's draughtsmanship made an impact on architects for its cold, literal qualities. The drawings were clear and easy to copy; they were not, however, very captivating for they were ruled in black pen, without washes or shadows, and the landscape surroundings were uninviting. The pupils in his office used a jagged T. square with which to rule in the tiling and brickwork.

4 Richard Norman Shaw. Design for the principal elevations at Merrist Wood, near Worplesdon, Surrey, for Charles Peyto Shrubb, 1876-1877. Pen and coloured washes on tracing paper (470 x 690).

This design combined tile-hanging, Bargate stone, half-timbering and brick in a random picturesque manner. The high chimney-stack expresses the inglenook behind it and immediately flanks the entrance bay on the front elevation — a trick of composition taken up repeatedly later, for example by Gerald Horsley at Balcombe Place, Sussex, and by Lutyens at Deanery Garden (see figure 52).

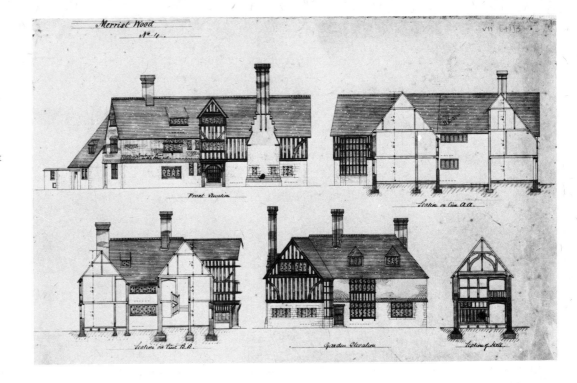

5 Richard Norman Shaw. Detail of entrance porch, Merrist Wood, 1876. Insc: *The spaces between / the timbers are / to vary slightly / as figured. The timbers / also are to vary slightly / in width.* Pen and coloured washes on tracing paper (510 x 735).

This working drawing of the front door shows the method of detailing in the Shaw office which was very similar to Arts and Crafts work. It shows the use of oak, pegging, leaded panes, brick infill, some set diagonally, and stone. Frank Birch was the builder, as he was also for Boldre Grange, Wispers, Pierrepont and Piccards Rough — all 'Old English' houses.

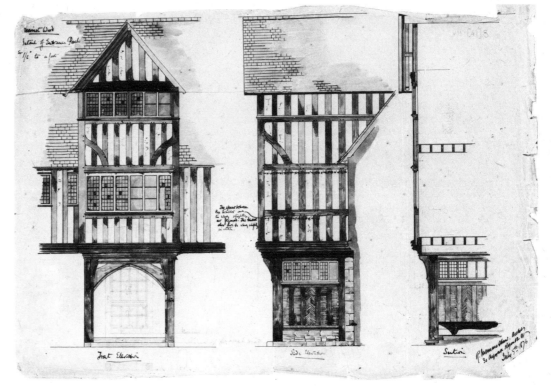

more modest scale. Here was a much more immediate example of a mixed vernacular style that Shaw's young Arts and Crafts men must have experienced detailing in his office. Shaw developed a method of using interchangeable details of which the RIBA has many examples. Details of window frames for Merrist Wood were inscribed 'to be in same detail as that at Pierrepont'; a detail for the porches at Wispers and Merrist Wood is identical and the panelling at Merrist Wood was to be the same as at Upper House, Shamley Green. Pierrepont's bargeboards were to be 'all similar to Wispers — or Boldre Grange — or any of our best specimens'.

This could be seen as standardisation or an attempt to leave the craft detail to the local builder — an Arts and Crafts principle. That Shaw was interested in the subtlety of vernacular detailing is very evident. A detail for the Library chimney at Piccard's Rough is inscribed 'brick and stone with / a few courses of tiles / here and there / Please make a very good / job of this so that / the brickwork may / appear to die gradually / into the stone work'.

Shaw's designs for 'Old English' houses had much Arts and Crafts spirit in them, but they were still, at the end of the day, very large in scale, 'Manorial' and 'Picturesque'. His commission to produce standard house designs for the new estate at Bedford Park in 1877 had far more influence on the new Movement, for the houses were moderate in size and for the middle classes. Semi-detached and detached, they were partly tile-hung, partly Queen Anne, and were very much the prototypes for later suburban housing developments. Only one faint pencil design for the first semi-detached house type exists at the RIBA, but the Collection has designs for the Stores, house and Tabard Inn (Fig. 6) and for the Church of St Michael and All Angels (Fig. 7), both designed by Shaw for the community at Bedford Park.

Yet, although it was the Shaw office, as we shall see, that provided the leading practitioners and campaigners in the Arts and Crafts Movement, it was Philip Webb's buildings that were more influential, and Philip Webb himself who provided the Movement's morality and theory. 'Architecture to Webb' W.R. Lethaby wrote 'was first of all a common tradition of

6 Richard Norman Shaw. Design for the Stores, house and Tabard Inn, Bedford Park, London, June 1879. Insc: *Please do not let the 'Building News' / get hold of this in its present state RNS.* Pencil (405 x 670).

Shaw's treatment of the facade of the Stores-Tabard Inn group, consisting of three separate units was a forerunner of the random town-vernacular treatment used by Ernest Newton in Bromley (see figure 21). Many individual features crop up again in later Arts and Crafts work: the Venetian window in the stores in Prior's The Barn, Exmouth, and Leonard Stokes's Shooter's Hill, Pangbourne; the expressed drainpipes recur constantly. The Tabard itself was a model Arts and Crafts building, with T.M. Rooke's inn sign, William De Morgan tiles in the bar and meeting room and Walter Crane reliefs.

7 Richard Norman Shaw. Design for the Church of St Michael and All Angels, Bedford Park, London, drawn by Maurice B. Adams, 1879. Pen (460 x 675).

A church that is almost like a church hall, St Michael and All Angels is a forerunner of what became a standard Arts and Crafts type. What was unusual in 1879 was its informal non-Gothic style, the 'arty' interior painted sage green and the mixture of Perpendicular and Wren detailing. The dormer windows in the roof later crop up in Lutyens's St Jude, Hampstead Garden Suburb. The perspective was drawn by Maurice B. Adams (1849-1933), architect and Editor of the *Building News*, the periodical that 'presented' all Shaw's Bedford Park designs — redrawn by Adams.

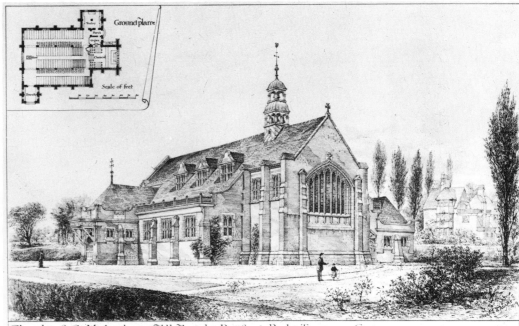

Church ·of· S ·Michael ·and· All ·Angels· Bedford ·Park· Tvrnham · Green · S·E· View · R· Norman ·Shaw· R·A·1880

honest building. The great architectures of the past had been noble customary ways of building, naturally developed by the craftsmen engaged in the actual works. Building is a folk art. And all art to Webb meant folk expression embodied and expanding in the several mediums of different materials. Architecture was naturally found out in doing; it is the very opposite of the whim "designs" we are so excited about exhibiting. In a word, architecture is building traditionally.'[2] The reason for Webb's influence was that his buildings provided examples of inventive ways of using traditional building crafts. Webb was solely interested in building craft and hence his buildings do not present a coherent style; nonetheless, his work was much visited and admired, in particular his vernacular work in Surrey. Joldwynds at Holmbury St Mary and Coneyhurst at Ewhurst must have been as popular in the 1890s as Le Corbusier's Villa Savoye and Garches were in the 1950s and 1960s. Philip Webb did not publish or exhibit but his influence was projected through SPAB which at that time was a 'school' of traditional building construction. His closest followers were Ernest Gimson, Alfred Powell, the Barnsley brothers, Thackeray Turner, Detmar Blow, W.R. Lethaby, and C.C. Winmill and John Hebb who carried Webb's influence with them when they joined the newly formed LCC Architects' Department. Others too, like Leonard Stokes and E.J. May came into contact with Webb's work through Architectural Association excursions arranged by Hugh Stannus.

Webb never received any premium-paying pupils into his office but he employed assistants to help him, one or two at a time, notably George Jack and William Weir. Webb designed every detail himself, to the smallest moulding, and his drawings are outstanding in as much as they are the first architectural drawings to convey elaborate and exact specifications about materials and craft. Shaw drawings are clear and have notes on materials but leave a lot to the builder. Webb's leave nothing to the builder. He knew everything about materials, and acted the part of the 'upper foreman' on paper. One revealing aspect of his drawings is the inscribed instructions to the builder, for example, on a working drawing for a staircase newel at Clouds House (No. 159): 'The carving to be / particularly done according to this design, keeping the curves / modelling, sections etc as here indicated. It should be clearly / and freely cut so as to give effect to the design as intended and / expressed by the drawing — clean-cut and effective tool-marks / to be left at completion, but no oversharp arrises to be / left in such a way as to be easily injured.'

Webb, shunning publicity, had wanted to burn all his architectural drawings when he retired to Sussex in 1900. Fortunately they were saved by Emery Walker, George Jack and Charles C. Winmill and later deposited in the RIBA and Victoria and Albert Museum, making him, ironically, one of the best documented architects. This would have pleased Lutyens who openly (and uncharacteristically) admitted his debt to Webb. Lutyens felt that 'it should be the duty of the present generation to make a faithful and technical record of his work, illustrated by his working drawings, specifications and even quantities, for there was no item in the fabric of his building too small or trivial for him to consider and design to fit its purpose.'[3]

The design for stables at Coneyhurst (Fig. 8) and the working drawing for the moat bridge at Great Tangley (Fig. 9) are good examples of Webb's precise drawing style, the one very fine, in ink, the other in pencil. Webb built the main house, Coneyhurst, in 1884, and a cottage (1885), as well as the stables. The stables, timber and tile-hung, are a good example of his particular genius — 'building traditionally'. One might even pass them by unnoticed, and no doubt Webb would have been delighted. In September 1885 Webb wrote to his friend Boyce: 'Miss Ewart has got into her house and seems to like it well enough, & when she gets some pretty things to grow against & veil the brickwork, I shall like it better.'[4]

Webb's work at Tangley Manor in 1885-1887 consisted of the restoration and extension to an existing fifteenth century farmhouse and a new covered way crossing the moat by a bridge. The covered way and bridge, with its structure openly expressed, and oak left unplaned, had enormous influence on Lutyens (notably at Pasture Wood and his bridge at Plumpton Place), on Herbert Baker, Ernest Gimson (Bedales Library) and a host of lychgates, pergolas and verandahs in England. Pevsner and Nairn (*Surrey*) note that his work at Tangley Manor was 'one of the first 19th century additions to an existing house to attempt to reproduce the spirit and deliberately avoid reproducing the letter of the old work.'

Ever since the decorating firm Morris, Marshall, Faulkner & Co had been founded in April 1861, with Webb as one of the partners, Philip Webb had designed many of the animals and birds for stained glass, tapestries, wallpapers and tiles, and there are many of these designs in the RIBA Drawings Collection, notably for the Ionides Tapestry called 'The Forest' made by Morris & Co in 1887. But Webb also introduced naturalistic details of birds, flowers and animals into his buildings, as for example in figures 10 and 11.

Webb's design for Standen at East Grinstead for a solicitor, James Beale (1892), is more modestly conceived in style and form. It no longer has the monumental qualities of a country seat — as Clouds House had — but its features and materials are all drawn from local building traditions. The new block of the house is anchored to an existing farmhouse, Hollybush Farm, by a long line of roof under which one enters the entrance courtyard. The materials used are complex. On the garden front (Fig. 12), the ground floor is of stone;

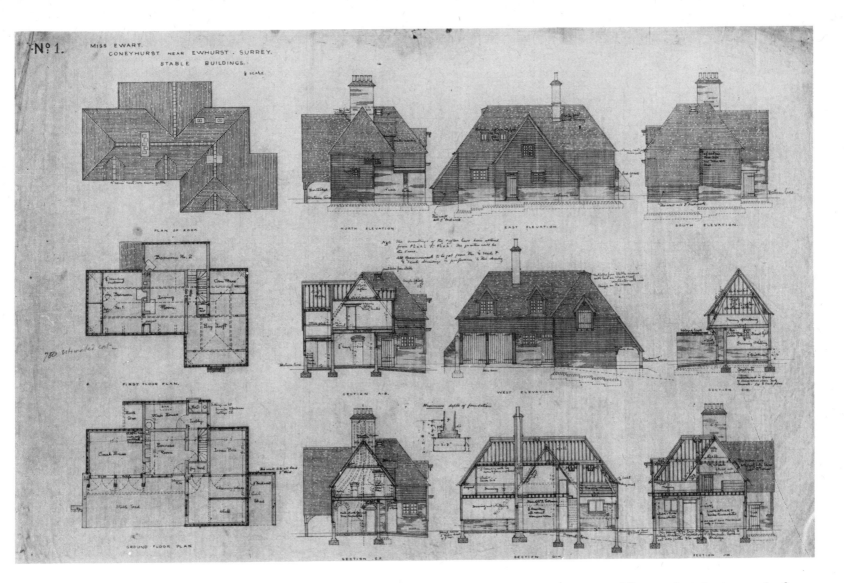

Nº 1.
MISS EWART.
CONEYHURST NEAR EWHURST. SURREY.
STABLE BUILDINGS.

8 Philip Webb (1831-1915). Design for stables at Coneyhurst, Ewhurst, Surrey, for Mary Ann Ewart, 1886. Pen and coloured wash on linen (520 x 760).

Coneyhurst, its stables and cottage were built from 1884-1886 by the builders William and George King of Abinger Hammer. Miss Ewart, a woman of independent means, was involved in the building of Newnham College, Cambridge, in the 1870s. The stables have now been converted into one dwelling called High Raise.

windows are set in brick surrounds, recessed on the ground floor and projecting on the first. Windows are separated by panels of tile hanging; coves are plaster; the five gables weather boarded; the wall above the conservatory is roughcast.

The design for cottages at Standen (Fig. 13) is a final example of a Webb working drawing, where different details drawn to different scales are combined on the same sheet, often recto and verso, showing his complete knowledge of craftwork and the control he had over a building.

Notes

1 e.g. Cotman's 'Cottage at St Alban's', Norwich Castle Museum, number 2366.

2. W.R. Lethaby *Philip Webb and his Work*, 1935, pp. 119-120.

3. E.L. Lutyens, 'The Work of the late Philip Webb', *Country Life*, XXXVII, 1915, p. 619.

4. Letter from Philip Webb to George Price Boyce (British Museum, MS 45354).

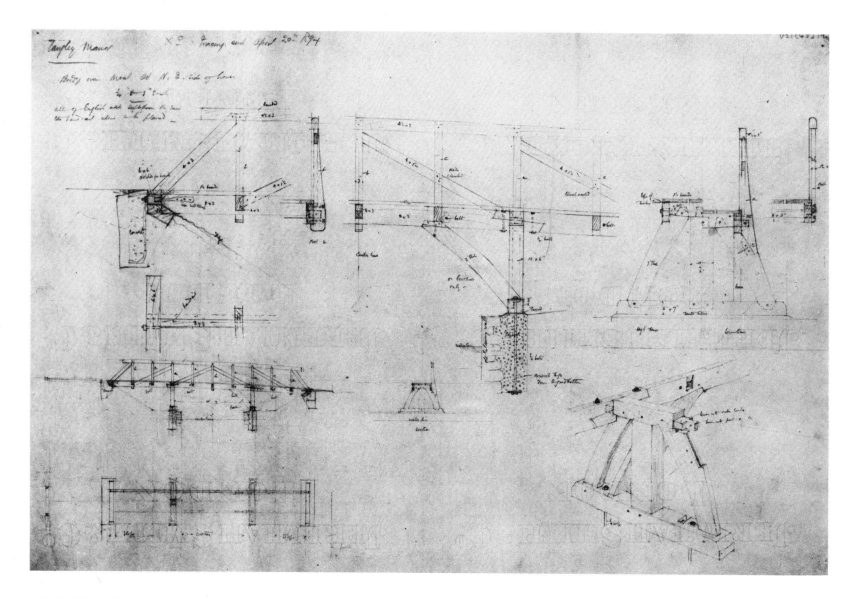

9 Philip Webb. Working drawing of the bridge over the moat at Tangley Manor, Great Tangley, Surrey, for Wickham Flower, 1894. Insc: *all of English oak left from the saw / the handrail alone to be planed.* Pencil (515 x 755).

10 Philip Webb. FS detail of carving over fireplace in west drawing room at Clouds House, East Knoyle, Wiltshire, for the Hon. Percy Wyndham, c.1886. Pencil with black crayon and white chalk on grey paper (635 x 495). This fireplace has now been destroyed.

11 Philip Webb. Working drawing for the gravestone to William Morris in the churchyard of St George, Kelmscott, Oxfordshire, for Mrs Jane Morris, 1897. Pencil and grey wash (775 x 985).

The tomb has a coped top like a house roof and was inspired by a piece of fourteenth century stonework lying in Kelmscott churchyard — 'to follow a local lead and improve upon it'. The oak saplings 'grew' up the centre of each coping, with the lettering in the south west panel. The carving was executed by Lawrence Turner, brother of Thackeray Turner, who did most of the decorative carving for Webb's buildings. Mr Giles, the gardener at Kelmscott Manor, was brought in to dig the holes for the foundations. Morris was carried in a farmcart to his grave.

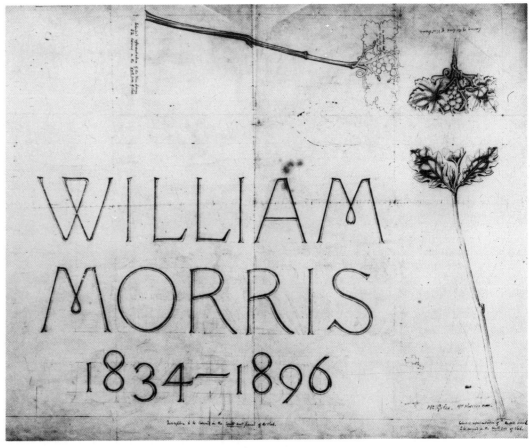

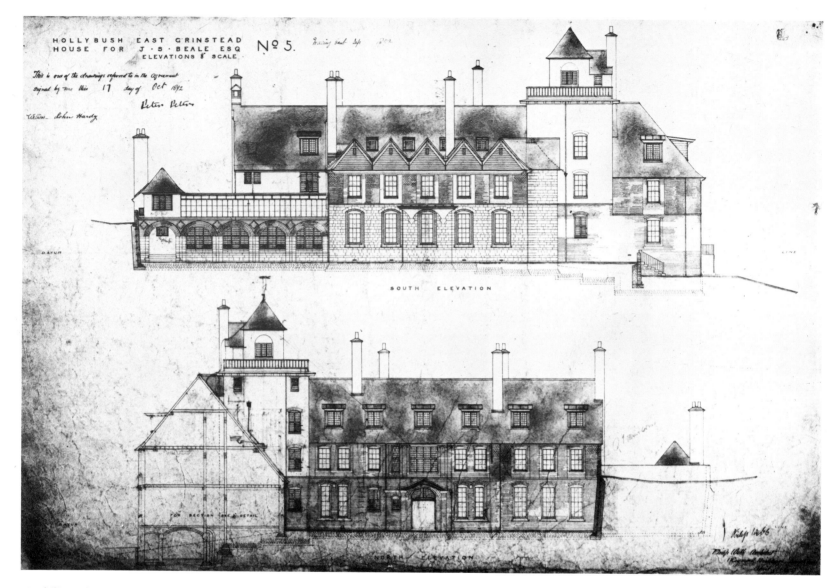

12 Philip Webb. Contract design for Standen
(formerly Hollybush), near East Grinstead,
Sussex, for James S. Beale, 1892. Pen and
coloured wash (505 x 745).

Standen was built by the contractor Peter Peters
of Horsham. There are 75 designs extant at the
RIBA and further drawings at Standen, which is
now owned by the National Trust.

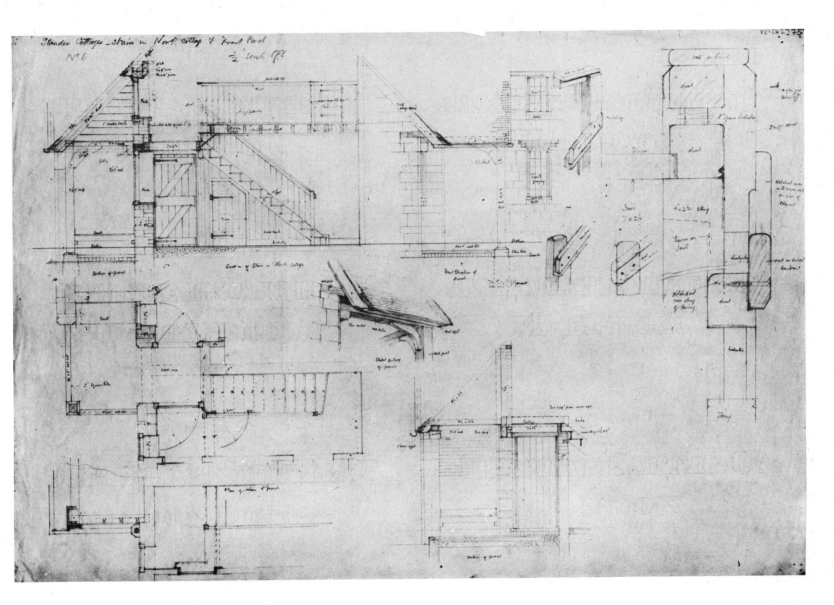

13 Philip Webb. Design for a pair of semi-
detached cottages at Standen, East Grinstead,
Sussex, for James S. Beale, 1896. Plans, elevations
and sections of porch and staircase, North
cottage, with small explanatory perspective sketch
of porch and details of staircase balustrade.
Pencil with some red pen (515 x 765).

14 Edward John May (1853-1941). Sketch of the interior of the Bull's Head, Ewhurst, Surrey, 29 May 1886, from Sketchbook I, p. 117. Pencil (205 x 165).

The inglenook sketched here was a good example of a prototype felt to be fast disappearing in the 1880s and 1890s. Home life, functionally as well as spiritually, was settled round the fireside. This fireplace has the heavy oaken beam used as a shelf and to suspend a short curtain to regulate the draught. Note also the inglenook seat, bellows and, in the hearth, the pair of wrought-iron cup-dogs. The branched tops held mugs of hot, spiced ale and the stems had ratchets with moveable hooks for the spit. May and many others of this period, notably Gertrude Jekyll in *Old West Surrey,* 1904, were interested in old Surrey objects of daily use, the designs of which were felt to be the best possible solutions for their varied purposes.

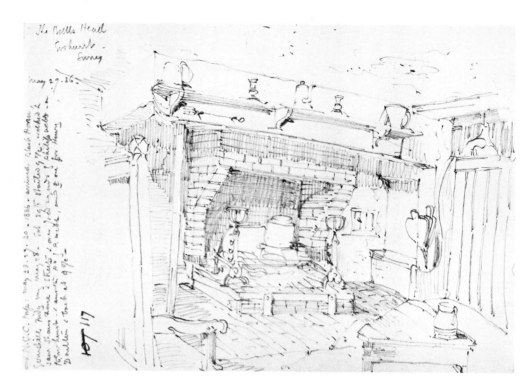

15 Edward John May. Sketch of candle holders (belonging to Mr Peter Aylwin of Haslemere), 25 July 1888, from Sketchbook II, pp. 10-11. Pencil (210 x 130).

Two kinds of candle holder are shown here. On the left, standing upright and laid across the bottom of the page, is the rush-light holder. Greased rushes are held in 'jaws' fixed in wooden blocks; counter-balance weights are formed into curls or knobs. Later, when tallow dip-candles came into use, the counter-balance was made into an actual candle-socket, as in the example on the right and laid across the page, centrally.

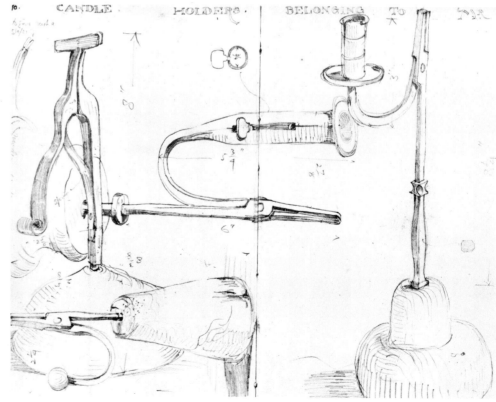

The Shaw Office

There was a quality in the Shaw Office that encouraged individuality. E.J. May, Mervyn Macartney, Ernest Newton, Gerald Horsley, E.S. Prior and W.R. Lethaby — to name his outstanding pupils (the remainder and office practice being fully described by Andrew Saint in *Richard Norman Shaw*, 1976) — all stayed with Shaw for some time, but left to set up their own individual and very different practices and to found and be the mainstay of the Art Workers' Guild, or to hold leading positions in the art establishment.

In Shaw's case, it was either his manner of gradually educating his pupils to take (small) design decisions, or his generosity in setting them on their feet with a good job, when they did want to leave, that encouraged this individuality.

Edward John May (1853-1941) entered the Shaw office in 1889, after being articled to Decimus Burton. The office was still at Argyll Street at this time, with Shaw and Nesfield sharing assistants although their partnership had ended. May was 'a charming and humorous man' and an excellent draughtsman, modelling his style of sketching exactly on Nesfield's. He stayed with Shaw until 1881 when he set up on his own largely to work on a 'plum' job from the office — Bedford Park. He designed several houses there, notably Nos. 15-25 Queen Anne's Grove (1883) and a house for a Dr Hogg in Priory Gardens (1883), as well as the Club (1878) and Vicarage (*c.* 1882). His practice from 1881-1929 was almost entirely domestic in character as throughout his career he refused to take part in any competition or take on any public work, though he was for many years architect to the Church of England Waifs and Strays Society. He was a fervent Art Workers' Guild member, and his own work scrapes into the Arts and Crafts category through its vernacular styling, although it was vernacular on a grand scale, and often Elizabethan manorial in style, as for example Barnsdale, near Oakham, Rutland, of 1890. But he was an inveterate 'scrambler' and organiser of scrambles, and it is interesting that he chose to bequeath to the RIBA only three of his sketchbooks, a Nesfield sketchbook, and his Pugin Studentship measured drawings of 1876. Sketchbook I is inscribed inside the cover, 'Half a word fixed on the spot is worth a cartload of recollection, Gray', and contains exquisite sketches made from 1876-1888 in England and on the Continent. A note on page 117 (Fig. 14) gives an idea of a typical trip, visiting contemporary buildings, but only actually sketching the old Surrey vernacular: 'N.C.C. trip: May 28.29.30 1886 — arrived Black Horse Gomshall Friday evg May 28. Sat 29th started 9 o/c walked & saw Shaw's house and Street's and over Joldwynds by Philip Webb — on to Ewhurst and another Ho by P. Webb, and one for Henry Doulton & back at 9 o/c.' (Visiting Shaw's Burrows Cross, Street's Holmdale, Joldwynds by Webb, Coneyhurst by Webb and Woolpit by Sir Ernest George and Peto).

His sketchbooks are filled with all the right details and the right buildings: oak coffers, old Surrey crafts (Fig. 15), sundials, oak pegging, timber roofs, Ledbury Town Hall and Stokesay Castle. Sketchbook I, page 138, has a copy of a Nesfield sketch of 'The Shop at Speldhurst', Kent, made in June 1863 and copied from the Nesfield sketchbook that May bequeathed to the RIBA. It was given to him by Mrs Nesfield in 1888. May continued to sketch. Lutyens writes[1] that May wanted to take him to the Art Workers' Guild — no doubt to encourage Lutyens to become a member, which he did do in that year — and wanted to know what he had built in Kent and Sussex so that he could show his son. In 1905 May again arranged a trip for the Guild, this time to see Lutyens's Deanery Garden at Sonning.

16 Ernest Newton (1856-1922). Contract design for the Bailiff's cottage at West Stratton, Hampshire, 1880. Sepia pen and coloured washes (530 x 670).

This design for a two-storey gabled cottage with verandah and bay window, made of brick and flint, plaster, oak and tile, was one of Newton's first jobs after leaving the Shaw office in 1879, and shows Shaw's influence in the high Tudor chimney, verandah details and projecting bay. However, it is also an early Arts and Crafts set-piece with its careful use of mixed local materials and hearts' motifs.

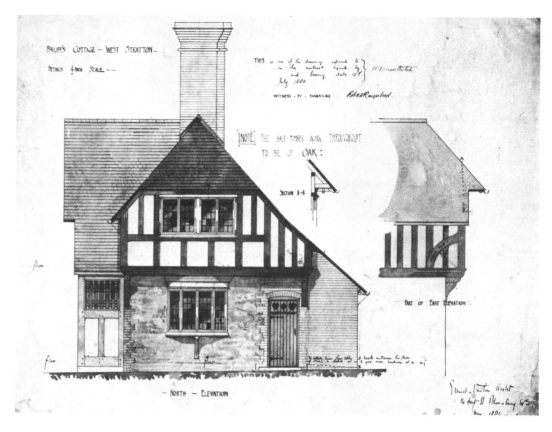

Ernest Newton (1856-1922) is very different. He was in the Shaw Office from 1873-1879 and, although his early work is very much like Shaw's (Fig. 16), his body of work was extremely influential and he was more than just a 'simplifier of the Shaw tradition'. He created a manner of practice that became standard until the Second World War, alternating between the Georgian and vernacular styles for country houses, a practice very much taken up by Lutyens and Guy Dawber in the 1900s but started by Newton in the early 1890s.

An extension to a mid-Victorian villa, Buller's Wood, Bromley, (Fig. 17) for a Bromley merchant, was Newton's first important domestic commission. Although stylistically the details are a fusion of Tudor and Georgian, and not vernacular, what links Newton to the Arts and Crafts Movement (he was also a founder member of the Art Workers' Guild) is his method of designing in broad, plain masses. It represented a great simplification of the Shaw manner. The drawing for Buller's Wood was exhibited at the Royal Academy in 1890, and the *Builder* noted, most perceptively: 'One ought to have a plan to appreciate this drawing, which merely represents a part of the garden side (apparently) of a house, with no indication of the meaning of the drawing. It is a remarkably good specimen of picturesque effect produced in pen line, accompanied by an apparently studious avoidance of anything that can be called architectural detail. There is no doubt a reticence in this which is expressive of home-like repose and is in good taste in a negative sense; it is a fancy with a certain school of architects at present to design houses with a studious avoidance of design, and this very negative quality gives such designs a certain recognisable and individual stamp of their own.'[2] Certain details were, however, very much Newton's own particularly the simplified, faceted bay. The interior (Fig. 18) shows a lovely light effect with decoration by Morris & Co.

Although much criticised as 'an ominous house with sterile Neo-Georgianism just round the corner',[3] Redcourt, Haslemere (Fig. 19) shows Newton's interest in vernacular-Georgian; an interest that would be regarded as perfectly legitimate by the Arts and Crafts Movement. Muthesius notes that Redcourt 'illustrates Newton's plain, broad, austere manner and its general appearance is an ideal example of what is called in England today a good house.'[4] He attributes much of Newton's (and Lethaby's) success to the 'masterly way in which the qualities of the material are handled and shown to advantage, the excellent work in every material, the subtle juxtaposing of colour in the different materials'.[5] It is possible that one of the reasons why Newton's work may be underestimated at present is that these qualities cannot easily be appreciated in photographs. His own sketches, however, do convey his interest in materials and the nature of rural, textured, red-brick Georgian far better than drawings by his perspective artists.

Newton's interest in 'locality character', traditional building methods and craft processes is again shown in his design for a group of buildings in Bromley High Street. Newton's own sketch for the bank (Fig. 20) shows far better than Raffles Davison's monumental perspective

17 Ernest Newton. Perspective, drawn by W.R. Lethaby, of the garden front of Bullers Wood, Bickley, Bromley, Kent, for Mr Sanderson, 1890. Pen (480 x 620).

This drawing, by Lethaby, emphasised the materials: the rough brickwork, the carving in the cornice, the drainpipe and sparkle of casements. The *Builder* considered the chimneys to be without finish.

18 Ernest Newton. Perspective drawn by
T. Raffles Davison of the interior of the Drawing
Room at Bullers Wood. Sepia pen (465 x 615).

The Drawing Room was decorated by Morris &
Co. The woodwork was painted white. Morris
himself stencilled the beamed ceiling with a
scarlet pimpernel pattern in buff, green and
pink.

19 Ernest Newton. Preliminary design, in
Newton's own hand, for Redcourt, Haslemere,
Surrey, for Louis Wigram, 1894. Sepia pen, pink
gouache, pink and green crayon on tracing paper
(340 x 510).

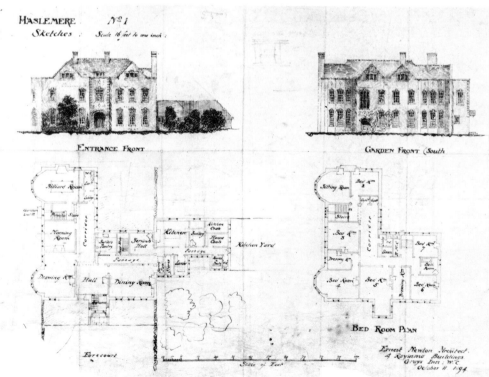

20 Ernest Newton. Design, in Newton's own hand, for Martin's Bank, Bromley, Kent, 1896. Sepia pen, green, red and yellow crayon and pencil on tracing paper (290 x 240).

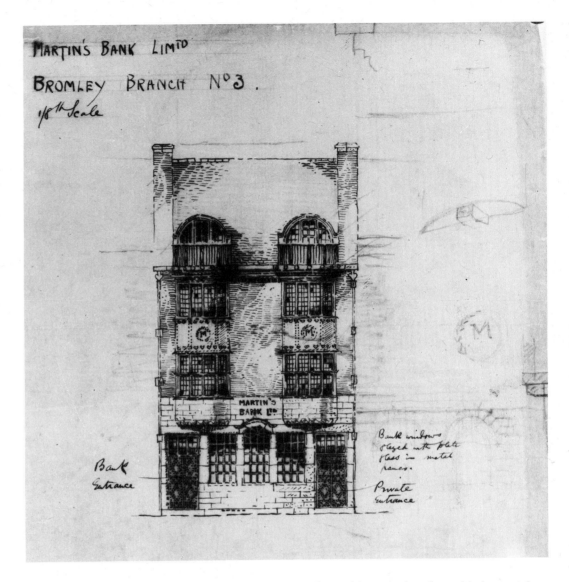

(Fig. 21) the modest town-vernacular scale he wanted to achieve. It also shows his interest in materials and crafts.

Newton's work was mainly domestic, and throughout his career was either vernacular in style and built from local materials or Georgian, stone or roughcast with bowed bays and shutters, like Steephill, Jersey. These houses were always substantial, although Newton could work on a smaller scale. Between 1899 and 1914 he designed the schoolmaster's house, cottages and farm buildings at Overbury, Worcestershire, and his design for a group of workers' cottages at Port Sunlight (Fig. 22) are pioneering in their planning and 'garden city' character.

Fouracre (Colour plate II) and Newbies (Fig. 23) are, however, more characteristic of Newton's work. Fouracre, particularly, epitomises his unmannered vernacular style that gives the impression of a building that has been rooted in the countryside for a couple of hundred years.

21 Ernest Newton. Perspective drawn by
T. Raffles Davison, of No. 181 High Street,
Martin's Bank and Bell Inn, High Street,
Bromley, Kent. Pen (660 x 975).

22 Ernest Newton. Perspective drawn by
T. Raffles Davison, of cottages at Port Sunlight,
Cheshire, for the Lever Brothers *c.* 1897. Sepia
pen (375 x 545).

A group of seven attached cottages, built of
stone, brick and tile. Each house had three
bedrooms, a living room, scullery, pantry and
bathroom, with an outside W.C. in the back
yard.

23 Ernest Newton. Perspective of the garden front of Newbies, Baughurst, Hampshire, for A.H. Lyell, drawn by T. Frank Green, 1903. Pen (495 x 630).

Although large (it has ten bedrooms), Newbies is a good example of Newton's white roughcast, asymmetrical vernacular manner that became very influential.

Gerald Callcott Horsley (1862-1917) was articled to Shaw in 1879, stayed on as his assistant, and left to set up a moderately successful practice of his own in 1889. He was the youngest son of the Victorian genre painter, J.C. Horsley, one of Shaw's closest friends, and consequently, in Lethaby's words, had 'inherited art'.[6] Architecturally, in style he was a close follower of Shaw's, but he was more of a craftsman than Shaw, more a genuine Arts and Crafts man. He was one of the founder members of the Art Workers' Guild and Lethaby thought that it was he and Macartney who actually originated the idea. 'I can recall', notes Lethaby, 'Horsley bringing exciting accounts of his calls on Burne-Jones and Morris and Crane and Sedding, and then the thing consolidated at a meeting held at Charing Cross Hotel. All this was accomplished with great skill, and it was a wonderful piece of work for so young a man.'[7]

Horsley had contributed an essay 'The Union of Art' to the volume of controversial essays, *Architecture, a Profession or an Art?*, in 1892. The theme of his essay was the attempt to merge the arts of painting, decoration and carving with architecture, the general principle underlying the foundation of the Art Workers' Guild. Consequently all Horsley's works are characterised by a similar love of carved decoration. Added to that he was seen as one of the ablest architectural draughtsmen of his time, and was constantly used as a perspective artist. Arthur Keen remembered that 'he could draw intricate vaulting or tracery with the utmost precision and firmness, or he could make beautiful studies of sculptured detail in which the most sensitive accuracy was combined with soft, refined texture.'[8] He did a good deal of watercolour work, but most of his drawings are in line, either in pencil or ink. Horsley was the first to win the RIBA's Owen Jones Travelling Studentship, from 1887-1888, visiting Italy and Sicily. In 1888 he drew the vestibule of La Zisa, Palermo (Fig. 24), as Aitchison and Burges and Viollet-le-Duc had done before him.

Shaw was good to Horsley (as he was to all his men), giving him work 'to begin with' when he set up on his own, and afterwards too. Horsley's metier was church decorative work, and

many of his jobs were decorative work in Shaw churches, as, for example, the painting of the chancel and design of fittings at All Saints, Leek, (Colour plate III) and the painting of the nave at the Church of St Swithun, Bournemouth (Colour plate IV). Shaw saw that Horsley was much better than he was at applied decoration and wrote commending him to Fred White for the chancel panelling at Swanscombe in Kent — 'I do think you could do ever so much better with a man more used to that sort of work. I always feel in all sincerity that church decorative work is not my metier . . . I am not quite at home in it. I date from the "Gothic" of 50 years ago, and the modern man does much better . . .'[9] In 1912 Horsley executed the organ case, chancel panelling and reredos at Swanscombe, a Shaw church of 1893.

Horsley's drawing of the Chancel screen at Ipstones (Fig. 25) is an example of his most typical drawing style: black pen marvellously presenting the natural carved decoration. Goodhart-Rendel called Horsley a 'fine draughtsman. He had a scratchy line but a wonderful sense of tone. He was the typical amateur but did much better work than usual among amateurs.'[10]

24 Gerald Callcott Horsley (1862-1917). Topographical drawing of the Hall at La Zisa, Palermo, 1888. Pencil and coloured washes (500 x 300)

In 1888 Horsley visited Sicily and chose to sketch La Zisa, which had been the source of inspiration for George Aitchison's Arab Hall at Leighton House (1879). The Arab Hall, with its tilework by William De Morgan, sculpture by Boehm, mosaics by Walter Crane and overall design by Aitchison, very much represented Horsley's concept of 'The Union of Art', and illustrated the principles of the Art Workers' Guild. La Zisa, built in 1154-1166, is a Norman Castle showing the influence of Moslem Art. This drawing shows the vestibule which is rich in marble columns, mosaics of peacocks and stalactite vaults.

25 Gerald Callcott Horsley. Design for the chancel screen at the Church of St Leonard, Ipstones, Staffordshire, 1899. Pen (430 x 450). Exhibited at the Royal Academy, 1899.

26 Gerald Callcott Horsley. Design for the interior of the Music Room, Balcombe Place, Balcombe, Sussex, 1899. Sepia pen (420 x 550).

The architectural form of the music room, which was an extension to the existing manor of the 1850s by Henry Clutton, followed the Shaw style, the exterior bland neo-Tudor, with inglenook and bay window. But the decorative work inside, all carved in pale oak, and the placing of the organ on a light gallery, makes this one of the loveliest rooms of the Arts and Crafts Movement. The figures above the fireplace were not carried out, but were replaced by roses, lilies and irises. The builder was Albert Escourt & Son of Gloucester.

The Music Gallery: Balcombe Place. Gerald C. Horsley Archt.

Horsley's major building is St Paul's School for Girls, Hammersmith, of 1904, following Shaw's 'Wrenaissance' manner, but redeemed in the Arts and Crafts sense, by the carved decoration, panelling and organ of its Great Hall. Very similar in decoration is the interior of the Music Room at Balcombe Place, Balcombe in Sussex (Fig. 26).

Muthesius greatly admired William Richard Lethaby (1857-1931), and wrote 'the number of his houses is not large but all appear to be masterpieces'.[11] The reason for this singling out of Lethaby as the ablest of Shaw's pupils, in contrast to his extremely cursory treatment of Prior, is that Lethaby was not too revolutionary. He designed in broad, plain masses, as did Newton, but according to Muthesius 'continued the best traditions of English house building';[12] in other words, whereas in his details he was very much an Arts and Crafts man, in general form his houses followed the Shavian pattern.

The RIBA has drawings for all Lethaby's buildings except High Coxlease, as well as many sketchbooks and topographical drawings. The majority were presented by Mrs Grace Crosby in 1933, but those for the Brockhampton Church, Melsetter House and Stanmore Hall came from R. Weir Schultz. Schultz did not usually revere working drawings, seeing them as a means to an end, but felt differently about Lethaby's: 'I went through the drawings for Avon Tyrrell two days ago, and I will say that no practising architect could have gone more thoroughly into the working details for the building of that house than he did, even to the designing of the furniture. I do not know what will happen to the drawings; it would be a pity to destroy them. They alone are a monument to him.'[13]

27 William Richard Lethaby (1857-1931). Sketch of old houses in the High Street, Exeter, made in 1880, from Sketchbook 6, p. 32. Insc: *The Carving on the Friezes is Lions Hds / in an Arabesque.* Pen (180 x 120).

Lethaby was born at Barnstaple, Devon, and worked for a time with a local architect, Alexander Lauder. In 1879 he was invited into the Shaw Office to replace Ernest Newton, and remained there until 1889. An early sketch of 1880 shows his interest in a local sixteenth century vernacular town house with its elaborate carving and bay windows on brackets (Fig. 27).

When he first left Shaw, Lethaby augmented his income by making designs for Morris and Company for Stanmore Hall in Middlesex, 1889-1890 (Figs. 28, 29). It was probably at about this time, and through Gimson, that he met Philip Webb at SPAB. Webb became his hero and he later wrote his biography. In spite of Webb's influence, however, his first major work, Avon Tyrrell (1891-1893) for Lord Manners is more Shavian in form (Figs. 30, 31, 32). The scale — which is large — of windows and chimneys, with a quality of hardness, are very like Shaw's, whereas the plain outline and craftwork are Lethaby's own. There are 229 designs and working details extant for the house and all are in Lethaby's hand. The elevations, most delicately drawn, give the impression of a house more moderate in scale, more naturally textured than was in fact built. Instructions on the working drawings give many examples of Lethaby's design intentions: 'Note: Generally I like simple / straight forward fixing better than / "secret fixing". Do not object to / bradding showing nor even screws.'[14]

The opinion of a contemporary is interesting. The Scottish architect, Robert Lorimer, visited Avon Tyrrell in the late 1890s and told his friend R.S. Dods in Australia that it failed in the very particulars against which Lethaby raged; that everything was 'done in the office' and not 'worked out on the spot as in the old days afore time'.[15]

Lethaby's next commission was for The Hurst, Four Oaks, Sutton Coldfield (Fig. 33), a house whose austere simplicity is well expressed in the drawing.

During the mid 1890s Lethaby was much taken up with art education and in 1896 was appointed joint director, together with George Frampton, of the LCC's new Central School of Arts and Crafts. In 1898 came the commissions for Melsetter House on Hoy, Orkney, and also for Lethaby's only urban building, executed with a local architect Joseph Lancaster Ball (1852-1933), for the Eagle Insurance Offices, Birmingham (Fig. 34).

Lethaby's last work, the Church of All Saints, Brockhampton (Figs. 35, 36, 37), has been called 'one of the greatest monuments of the Arts and Crafts Movement',[16] and is certainly Lethaby's finest building. Here the architecture lived up to the romance of his theories.

It was constructed of local red sandstone, its forms deriving from local Herefordshire churches. The square crossing tower is very like Abbey Dore, the weather-boarded bell tower like the Pembridge bell-house. But there is also a hint of a vernacular structure: it could almost be a barn. It is roofed with a high pointed concrete vault covered by thatch, an interesting form of construction combining excellent insulation with fire resistance. The specification, dated April 1901 (at the RIBA), gives the method of work: 'The whole of the work to be done "Day Work" under a Clerk of Works [A. Randall Wells] and a general foreman appointed by Mr Foster of Brockhampton Court and all according to the architect's particular directions and detail drawings . . .' There are 11 drawings for the church at the RIBA and these, too, have changed in their method of presentation. Lethaby, in theory, was very against 'Art' architecture. He favoured the practice of the Middle Ages where 'art was so intimately bound up with production that their divisibility was never considered: everything was made in the customary way, just as a cook now makes pies; there was then no separate

continued on page 45

I George Devey (1820-1886). Contract design for cottages at Penshurst, Kent, 1850. Pencil and coloured wash (305 × 490).

The earliest known example in the RIBA Drawings Collection of a vernacular design by a Victorian architect, this drawing shows Devey's delicate watercolour technique. Thomas Barber was the local contractor. Voysey took over many of Devey's details, notably the roughcast jettying out and the water butt in this design.

II Ernest Newton. Perspective of Fouracre, West
Green, Hampshire, drawn by Thomas Hamilton
Crawford, 1902. Pencil and watercolour
(250 × 370).

This design shows Newton's straightforward use
of traditional building materials. It is built of red
brick, with ornamental diaper bands of red and
grey bricks and tiles; it has shuttered sashes to
distinguish the reception rooms and lead
casements for the remainder. The scale is,
however, deceptive, for the house has nine
bedrooms.

III Gerald Callcott Horsley. Design for the interior decoration of the chancel, Church of All Saints, Leek, Staffordshire, 1891. Pen and watercolour (685 × 505).

Exhibited at the Royal Academy in 1891. The *Builder* (1891, 20 June, p. 487) commented — 'The nearer portion of the chancel wall is occupied by a Gothic-looking diaper ornament arranged on net work lines...near the trunk two angels stand under the foliage; the whole being treated in a quite flat and decorative manner. The roof timbers are painted in a manner based on Mediaeval examples. The remainder of the decoration is original in design, and the colour effect of the drawing has a decided character of its own.' All Saints was a Shaw church of 1885-1887.

IV Gerald Callcott Horsley. Design for the painted decoration of the North Wall of the nave at the Church of St Swithun, Bournemouth, Hampshire, 1909. Pen and watercolour (585 × 355).

Exhibited at the Royal Academy, 1909. The church was designed by Shaw in 1876.

V Edwin Lutyens. Sketch design for The Hut (now Munstead Wood Hut), Munstead, near Godalming, Surrey, for Gertrude Jekyll, 1892. Insc: *Abandoned Oct 9th / 1892 / Restored to favour / July 16th 93*. Pen and watercolour (115 × 175). From the 'Munstead Wood Sketchbook'.

The Hut is an exact recreation of a vernacular Surrey cottage, tile-hung with a hipped roof and corbie-stepped chimney. At one end there is an open-roofed living room with large inglenook fireplace, but only three other small rooms downstairs and two bedrooms upstairs. The casement windows are oak-framed with pegging.

The Hut was so exact in its evocation of Surrey that Gertrude Jekyll included a photograph of it in *Old West Surrey*, 1904, to illustrate the use of cluster roses in old cottage gardens. At the Hut Miss Jekyll could recreate the comparative simplicity of an 'Arts and Crafts' life: she had one servant with her who slept upstairs, whereas she slept below, her bed on the 'brick floor, without carpet'.

VI John Dando Sedding. Full-size design for the decoration of a fireplace. Pencil and watercolour (760 × 1750).

This drawing is possibly a design for the painted decoration of a fireplace surround — most probably for a bedroom fireplace as the owls, poppies, woody nightshade, moths and stag beetle all symbolise Night and Sleep.

VII Henry Wilson. Design for the extension of the Church of St Bartholomew, Ann Street, Brighton, Sussex, *c.* 1898. Interior perspective showing the new high altar and baldacchino against an openwork screen beyond which is seen the Lady Chapel with, high up on its East Wall, a mural of the Mother of God in Glory. Charcoal, gouache and watercolour (1340 × 780).

It was intended to pierce the east wall of the church and turn it into an openwork screen, then continue the main structure for three bays to form a Lady Chapel. The new east wall was to be covered with a mural (presumably mosaic) representing the Mother of God in Glory, about thirty feet high. The chapel was to be barrel-vaulted, with convex coving. The effect is overwhelmingly Byzantine and Nicholas Taylor notes that the architectural painter William Walcot used the baldacchino and other details in his painting *Justinian weds Theodora*, the architecture, of course, being that of Hagia Sophia. All that was carried out, however, from 1899-1908, was the baldacchino with the altar and its fittings, pulpit and the giant candlesticks.

HOUSES·AT·FROG
NAL·HAMPSTEAD·
FOR·T·I·COBDEN-
SANDERSON·AND·
REGINALD·BLOM-
FIELD·1892·

·THE·PLAN·

VIII Reginald Blomfield. Design for Nos. 49-51 Frognal, Hampstead, London, for T.J. Cobden-Sanderson (no. 49) and for himself (no. 51), 1892. Pen and watercolour (460 × 620).

The design of this semi-detached pair of houses is close to Shaw's and E.J. May's houses at Bedford Park of the late 1870s; in its presentation, too, with its bird's-eye perspective, sign board and inset plan, it is reminiscent of Shaw's perspectives and, particularly, the set of coloured lithographs of Bedford Park by M.

Trautschold published in 1882. There are several consciously rural features: expressed drainpipes, side porches and hipped dormers, although when executed the houses appear grander in scale, with greater emphasis placed on their 'Queen Anne' gables and Venetian windows.

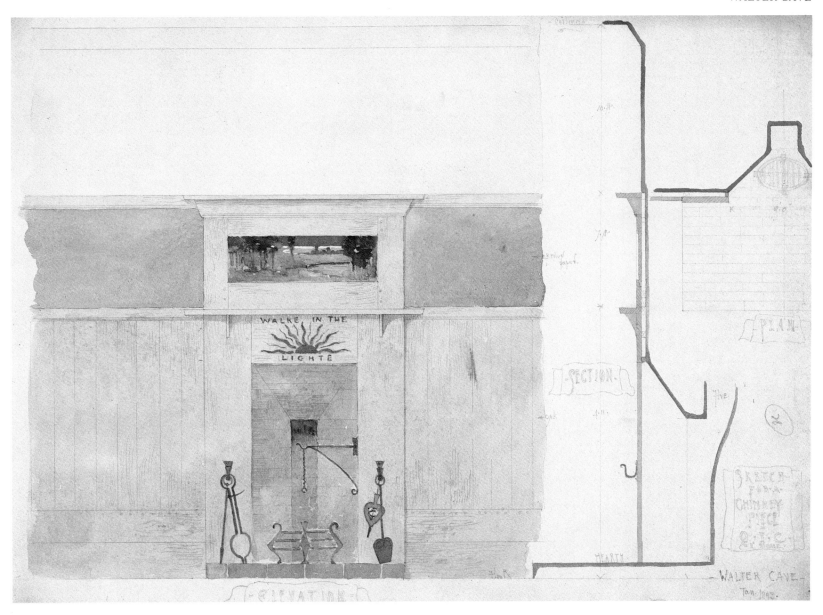

IX Walter Frederick Cave. Design for a chimneypiece, January, 1893, for the Quarto Imperial Club, Volume II, p. 28. Pencil and watercolour (280 × 395).

This design is drawn in a consciously naive manner. The style of the chimneypiece and its ironmongery are in the vernacular tradition; the surround, wall and panelling are of oak with pegging clearly shown. There is a painting above the fireplace, a carved inscription *Walke in the Lighte* above the sun's rays and plain brown paper above the panelling. The design shows the combination of natural materials and applied craft practised by the Arts and Crafts architects; the sheet is also laid out decoratively, with plan and section fitted in on the right hand side. The drawing was prepared for a Quarto Imperial Club meeting on the 25 January, 1893, when Voysey read a paper on chimneypieces.

X Charles Sydney Spooner (1862-1938). Design for the external treatment of a Town House, May, 1890, for the Quarto Imperial Club, Volume I, p. 13. Pen and watercolour (355 × 255).

Spooner's design is very original for its date, 1890. In its massing, and especially in the way the gable is combined with a conically projecting bay, it comes close to the work of the American architect H.H. Richardson and to the London houses of James MacLaren — Nos. 22 Avonmore Road, West Kensington (1888-1889) and 10-12 Palace Court, Bayswater (1889-1890) which have similar strips of carved decoration. The design is interesting in showing both Richardson's and MacLaren's influence on the younger architects of the Art Workers' Guild.

Sketch for the External treatment of a Town House.

Charles Spooner.

XI Charles Francis Annesley Voysey. Design for a coach house and stables at Moorcrag, near Windermere, Westmorland, for J.W. Buckley, 1900. Pencil and coloured washes and watercolour (780 × 560).

Voysey built this combined stables and coach house, with granary above, in rough local stone, only using roughcast for the end elevations. He uses one drawing to supply all the instructions for the builder. In the bottom half of the sheet are the designs, drawn to ⅛th scale: four elevations are rendered in watercolour, with plans, a section and two details in pencil of the stable door and window. In the top half are details to a larger scale, arranged around a section. Full watercolour is reserved for the elevations, whereas two plain colours, blue and yellow, are used for the working drawings. This gives the sheet great clarity and at the same time a primitive, rather decorative quality which was unusual in working drawings of this date.

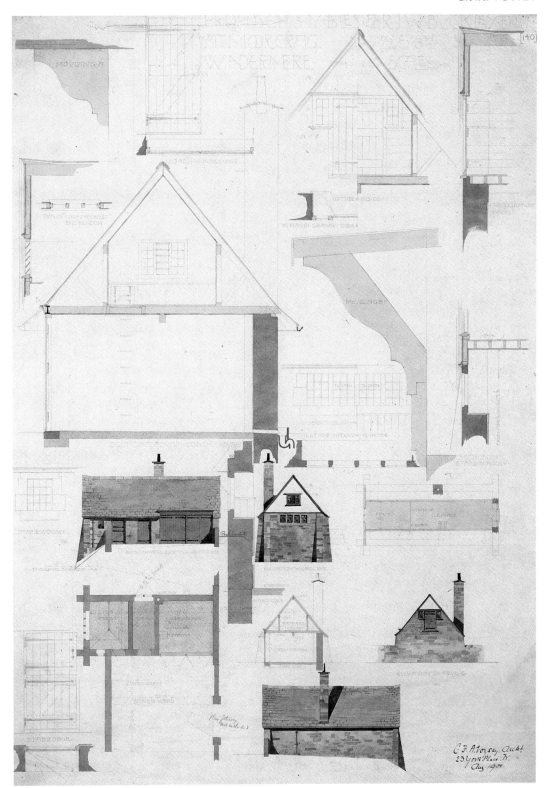

XII Charles Francis Annesley Voysey. Design for Oakhurst (now called Ropes and Bollards), Ropes Lane, Fernhurst, Sussex, for Mrs E.F. Chester, April 1901. Watercolour on card (255 × 375).

Oakhurst, like Voysey's house for H.G. Wells at Sandgate, is built into a steeply sloping site. In spite of this the long roof line is maintained over two parallel contiguous blocks running from east to west. The view in this drawing is of the north entrance front; the porch is approached from a courtyard, but the site then drops to form a lower garden on the west side. The double-height windows on the corner express a two-storey hall which was not eventually executed. Voysey himself painted this delicate watercolour perspective. It shows an idealised garden in April, with bluebells and daisies, painted with Voysey's 'human reverence for nature', there is a chill in the air and smoke coming from one of the chimneys gives a sign of human habitation. The tree in the left foreground is similar to those drawn in flat decorative patterns in his wallpaper designs. The house was built by F. Müntzer of 16 Dover Street and Godalming, a contractor much used by Voysey, in brick and roughcast with local stone terrace walls and steps and local red-tile roofs. The windows had bath-stone dressings and iron casements.

28 William Richard Lethaby. Design for the staircase, Stanmore Hall, Stanmore, Middlesex, for Morris & Company, *c.* 1890. Pencil and yellow crayon (500 x 330).

Stanmore Hall was rebuilt in *c.* 1890, and decorated by Morris & Company for William Knox D'Arcy.

29 William Richard Lethaby. Design for the fireplace, Stanmore Hall, *c.* 1890. Insc: *Alternative design for Fireplace / showing also the wall panelling / only 6'O" high: giving 8'6 to hangings / Marble & Carved Alabaster (coloured).* Pencil and crayon on tracing paper (290 x 370).

designer of art pies, making working drawings and writing specifications for their confection.'[17] This reflected the widely held view by craft architects that drawings and working details hampered the construction of a building by inhibiting the craftsmen.

Lethaby did not quite achieve this at Brockhampton, for he still produced the working drawings and specifications (although this is extremely general in its instructions and lacks detail). But there was no contractor, the work being let out as day work. There are, too, fewer drawings extant for Brockhampton. This may be chance, for many may be lost, although Lethaby's drawings, like Webb's, were assiduously collected by his friends. The drawings are tentatively, almost roughly, drawn. The preliminary design (Fig. 35) has lost the ink presentation of the Shaw office and is in faint pencil; the detail (Fig. 36) takes the form of a sketch: a skeleton diagram for the craftsman. The method of direct labour, however, and the responsibility it placed on him, was too much for Lethaby. He was brought to the verge of a breakdown and did not repeat the experiment.

Edward Schroeder Prior (1852-1932) was the most eccentric, intellectual and original pupil in the Shaw office. There are numerous anecdotes about his heartiness and strength of character — the best told by Reginald Blomfield: 'nothing was going to prevent Edward Prior from saying what he thought, and he did not think on commonplace lines'.[18]

Prior entered the Shaw office in 1874 and left to set up on his own in 1880, developing a small practice which virtually ceased in 1916 as in 1912 he had become the Slade Professor of

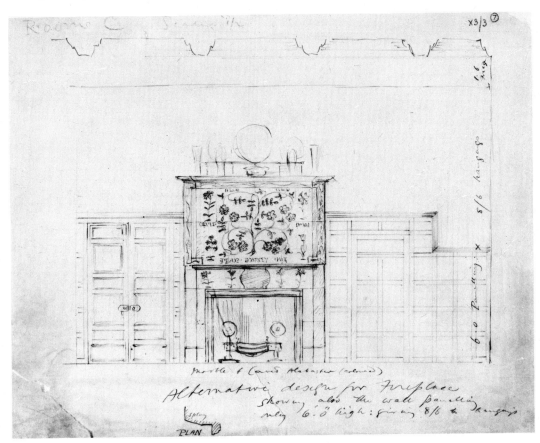

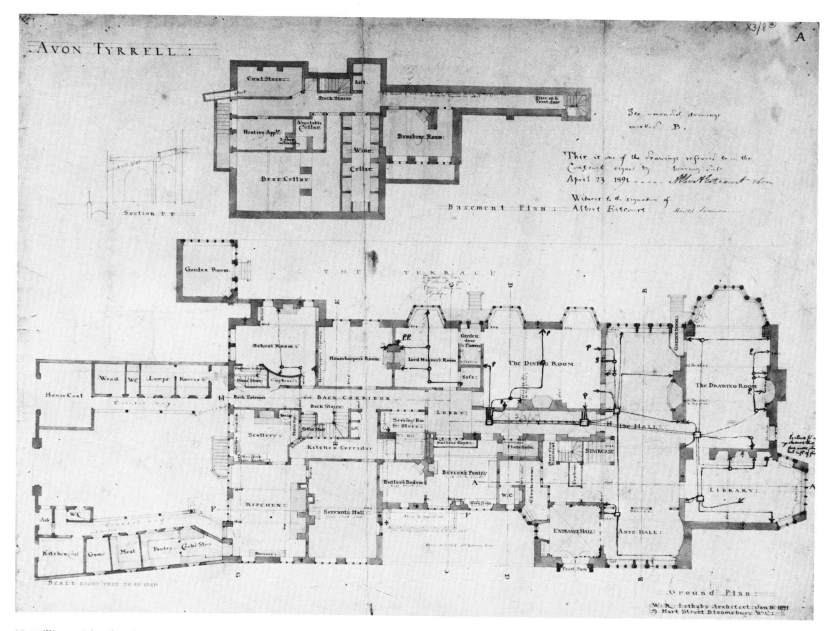

30 William Richard Lethaby. Contract design for
Avon Tyrrell, near Ringwood, Hampshire, for
Lord Manners, 1891. Basement and ground
plans. Pen and coloured wash (510 x 680).

The builder was Albert Escourt & Son from
Gloucester, nearly ninety miles away. The witness
to the signature was Harold Swainson, Lethaby's
collaborator on *The Church of Sancta Sophia
Constantinople*, 1894.

31 William Richard Lethaby. Revised contract design for Avon Tyrrell, 1891. Garden elevation. Pen, blue wash and red crayon (425 x 725).

This delicate drawing shows far better than the executed work Lethaby's Arts and Crafts intentions. Note the moulded lead-work on the bays (of a stag and the Manners' arms), expressed drainpipes, gables with bays positioned beneath their valleys, hearts' motifs and patterned stonework at the base of the massive chimney. The interior is all white, with decorative plasterwork by Ernest Gimson of 1892, and plain marble fireplaces.

32 William Richard Lethaby. Contract design for the stables at Avon Tyrrell, 1892. Insc: *Pebbles taken / out of site / tarred when done on face.* Pen and pencil with coloured washes (510 x 690).

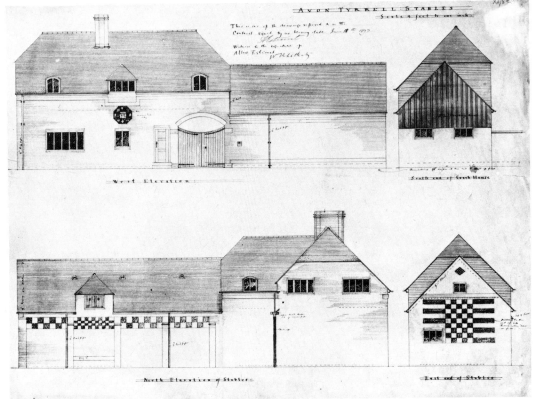

33 William Richard Lethaby. Contract design for The Hurst, Hartopp Road, Four Oaks, Sutton Coldfield, Warwickshire, for Charles Edward Matthews, 1893. Pen (680 x 510).

The kitchen wing, on the left, was defined by a vernacular hipped roof; the main block was gabled. It was built by James Smith & Sons of thin red Leicester bricks and roofed with hand-made tiles from Hartshill. The plasterwork of the Drawing Room was designed and executed by Ernest Gimson. The house has since been destroyed.

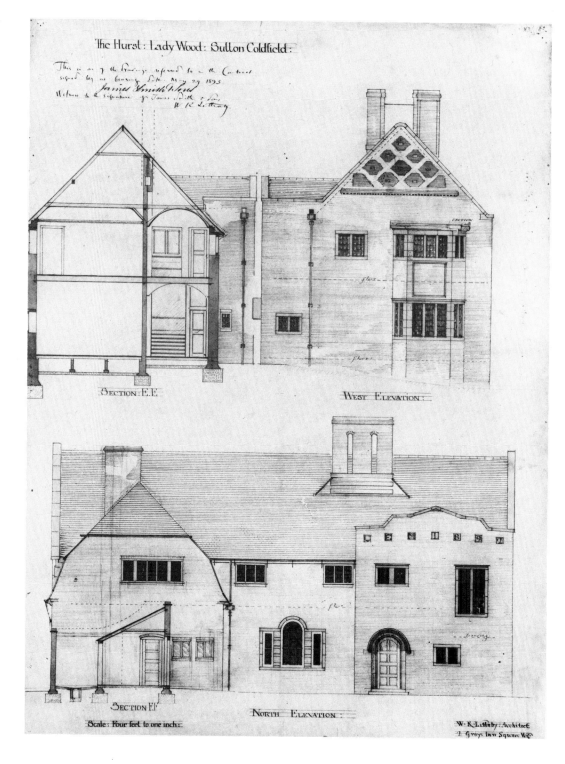

34 William Richard Lethaby and Joseph Lancaster Ball (1852-1933). Design for the Eagle Insurance Company Offices, Colmore Row, Birmingham, 1900. Pen and coloured washes (535 x 730).

The building is symmetrical on the exterior: a play on classicism, though a totally original classicism. The facade has three storeys of simplified columns and its symmetry is maintained by increasing the height of the doorway on the right. The major window springs straight from the ground. The top is extraordinary: a wavy cornice of alternating shapes, surmounted by mystic ornament — an eagle surrounded by circles and wavy lines, symbols of the sun and clouds. This design was executed, except that it shows the eagle standing proud of the sky line instead of against the closed parapet. It was one of the first buildings of this period in which lettering formed part of the general design.

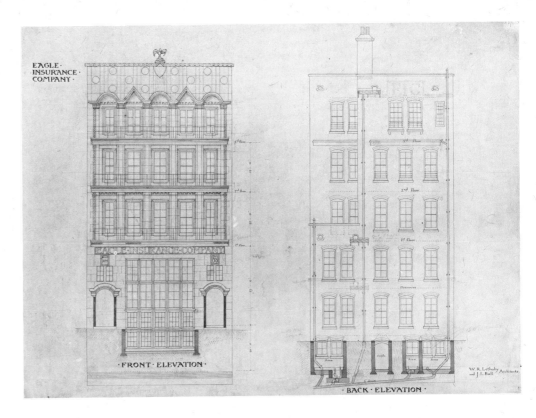

35 William Richard Lethaby. Preliminary design for the Church of All Saints, Brockhampton, Herefordshire, 1901. Insc (stamped): *Approved conditionally / Ecclesiastical Commissioners for England / 25 Apr 1901.* Pencil with grey, grey-green and sepia washes (515 x 690).

As executed the Church was roofed with thatch and not with tiles as in this drawing. The specification (in the RIBA), dated 29 April, requires thatch so Lethaby must have made the change very quickly. The stone came from quarries on the estate; the belfry was covered with oak feather-edge boarding.

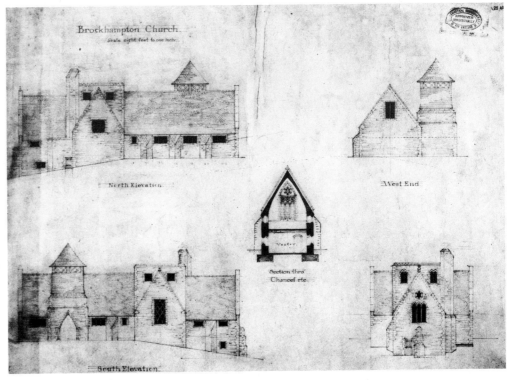

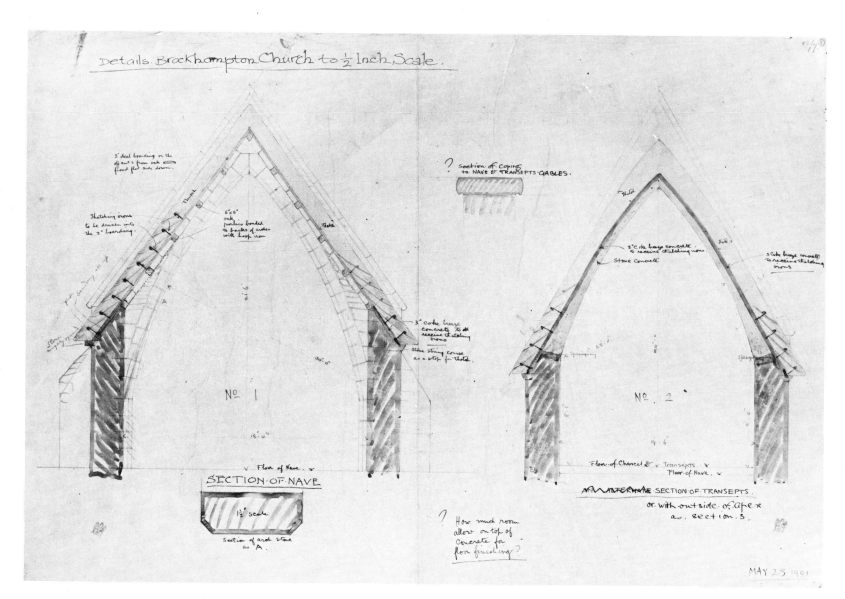

36 William Richard Lethaby. Working drawing
for Brockhampton Church: sections of nave and
transepts, 28 May, 1901. Insc. with notes on
construction, for example: *5″ x 5″ / oaks / purlins
bonded / to backs of arches / with hoop iron / 3″ coke
breeze concrete / to receive thatching irons.* Pencil and
pen with grey, green and yellow washes on
tracing paper (500 x 755). The thatch was laid on
concrete vaulting 'formed on rough boarding
laid on centering' (specification).

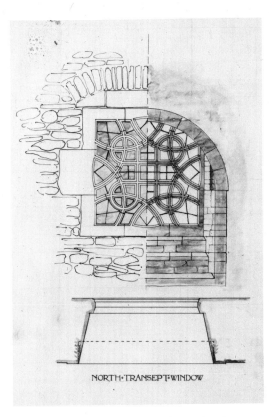

NORTH·TRANSEPT·WINDOW

37 William Richard Lethaby. Design for the north transept window, All Saints Church, Brockhampton, February 1902. Interior and exterior elevations and FS section. Pen and wash on tracing paper (445 x 510).

38 Edward Schroeder Prior (1852-1932). Design for Lodging Houses and the Lost Sailor Hotel, West Bay, Dorset, *c.*1885. Pen (405 x 530).

Although this design is in the Shaw office manner, there are many original features. The placing of plans and a perspective on the same sheet is not Shaw practice; there are also touches of whimsy in the superimposed and curled back plan and in the addition of figures in the perspective — not common in Shaw's work.

Fine Art at Cambridge and later founded the Cambridge School of Architecture. He was also a fine writer and historian, and published *A History of Gothic Art in England* (1900), which Gerald Horsley illustrated.

In comparison with Shaw and his four pupils already mentioned (May, Newton, Horsley and Lethaby), Prior's work is outstanding for its absence of period references. A founder member of the Art Workers' Guild, he was dedicated to its more revolutionary aims, stating his own theory — 'the "styles" are dead . . . such things are gone by. The savour of his art to the architect is no longer in knowledge but in experiment, in the devices of craftsmanship, in going back to the simple necessities of Building and finding in them the power of beauty.'[19] In the same way, Prior's drawings, as drawings, are equally revolutionary. They are also crucial documents as they help to expand our knowledge of Prior's small oeuvre for he did not publish regularly. He rarely used perspective artists, occasionally chose to present his houses in model form at the Royal Academy (rather bizarre), and worked on several schemes which were never executed. The RIBA acquired the collection of his drawings from Prior's daughter, Mrs Templar, in 1966.

By about 1890 Prior had shaken off Shaw's drawing mannerisms. That he could both draw well and design in the Shaw manner is clear from his unexecuted design of *c.*1885 for Lodging Houses and the Lost Sailor Hotel at West Bay, Dorset (Fig. 38), which in style is close to Shaw's Bedford Park Stores and Tabard Inn (see figure 6). Blomfield, incidentally, says Prior could not draw, something which this drawing disproves. By the early 1890s, however, Prior's

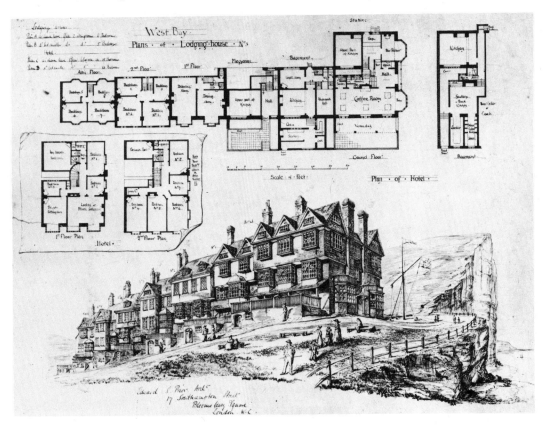

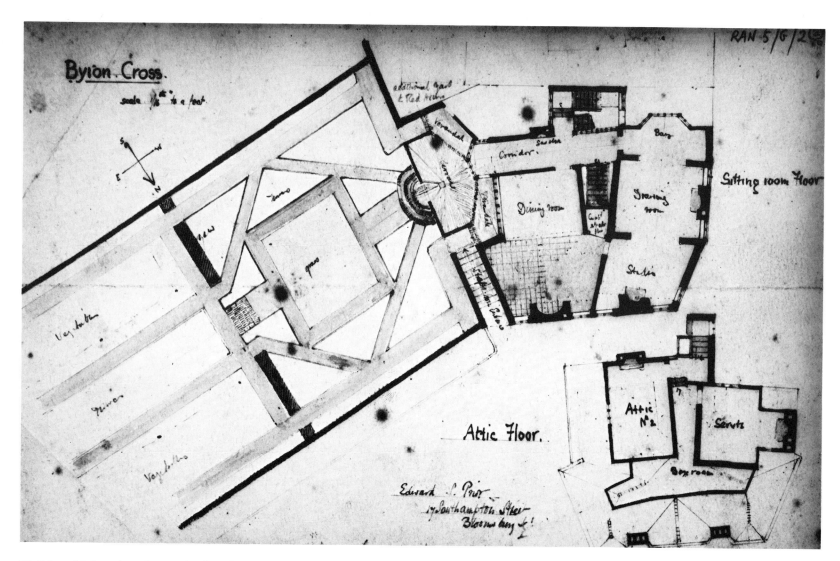

39 Edward Schroeder Prior. Design for a house,
Byron Cross, Byron Hill, Harrow, Middlesex,
1891. Attic and Sitting Room floor plans. Pencil
and coloured washes (160 x 260).

40 Edward Schroeder Prior. Elevations of Byron Cross, Byron Hill, Harrow, Middlesex, 1891. Pencil and coloured washes (160 x 260).

Sited next door to Prior's Red House, Byron Cross was never executed. These designs show how original the house would have been, growing from the hill, the plan asymmetrical and angled.

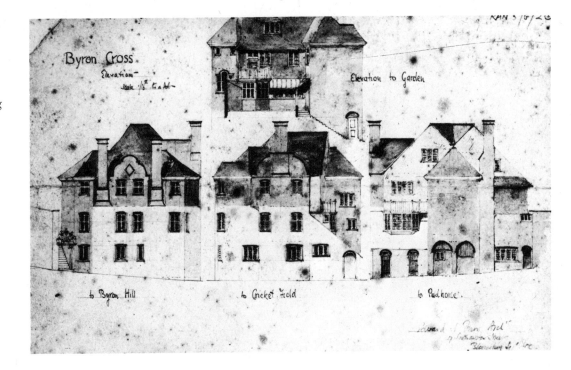

41 Edward Schroeder Prior. Unexecuted design for a Club, with covered promenade, swimming baths, tea room, shops, library, smoking and reading rooms, West Bay, Dorset, mid 1890s. Pen and watercolour (390 x 565).

These side elevations are the most revolutionary part of the design; the front elevation contained a pair of symmetrical Venetian windows. The roof was of green transparent felt.

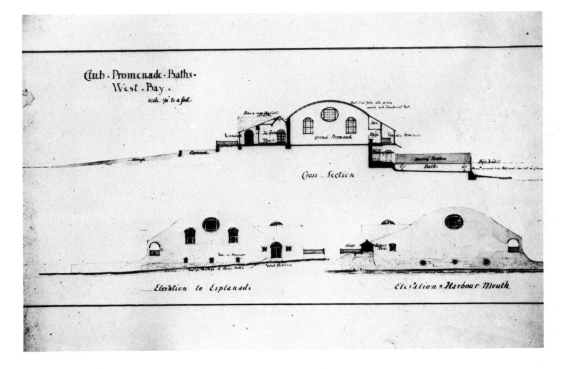

drawing manner becomes as astylistic as his buildings. His designs are obviously not drawn to look well on paper but simply to communicate facts, a theory often voiced by the architects of the Movement, particularly Randall Wells, Lethaby, Gimson and Lutyens. The method of drawing the house at Harrow, Byron Cross (Figs. 39, 40), and the West Bay swimming baths (Fig. 41) is without precedent. The handling is informal, delicate, the designs being presented unemphatically in pencil or pen with coloured washes.

Very few drawings exist for The Barn, Exmouth (1896), Prior's most influential building. There is a plan and a section at the Rolle Estate Office,[20] and another plan at the RIBA which was only drawn for publication. Indeed, one wonders if he did produce any details at all, for he believed that the architect should act as builder and specifier of materials without thought of design. He closely supervised the construction of The Barn, working from his father-in-law's rectory at Bridport. There are, however, contemporary photographs of models now lost, both exhibited at the Royal Academy, which are studies on the theme of the house.

The first, exhibited in 1895, is a model of a house in Dorset (Fig. 42) and is very close to the executed design for The Barn, although it is roofed with tiles and not thatched. It has the highly influential butterfly plan, the use of which came to be one of the hall-marks of the Arts and Crafts Movement. The second model (Fig. 43), exhibited in 1899, was made of wax and has a double-butterfly plan.

The Barn illustrated one of the dominant theories of the Movement: the use of local materials, 'Nature's own textures' as Prior called them, and the organic growth of the form of a building out of the landscape. Its walls were faced with pebbles from the nearest beach and dressed with sandstone; the roof was thatched with speargrass.

Again, no drawings are known to exist for Kelling Place (now Home Place), Holt, Prior's second and larger butterfly plan house of 1903-1905. This was built from materials dug on the

42 Edward Schroeder Prior. Contemporary photograph of a model for a house in Dorset, 1895.

The model was exhibited at the Royal Academy in 1895, which was an unusual step, especially as it was made of clay and rather roughly finished. The *Builder*, however, reacted rather well: 'It is comparatively rough in appearance and revolutionary in its tendencies. We do not like to suggest anything so much below the dignity of "professional" architecture but we strongly suspect Mr Prior of having made the model with his own hands. He is quite capable of it. Most interesting . . .' (*Builder*, 1895, p. 323).

43 Edward Schroeder Prior. Contemporary photograph of a model made of wax for a house of double-butterfly plan, 1899. The model was exhibited at the Royal Academy in 1899.

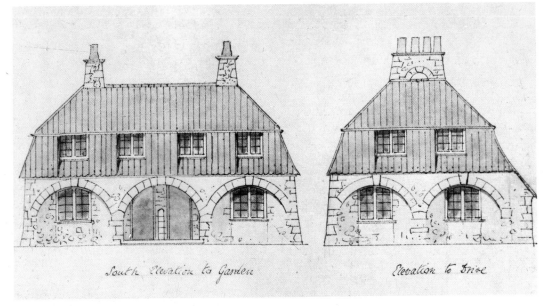

South Elevation to Garden

Elevation to Drive

44 Edward Schroeder Prior. Design for a pair of cottages at Kelling (now Home) Place, Holt, Norfolk, 1907. Pen and coloured washes (200 x 255).

site, with Randall Wells as site clerk. What the RIBA does have, however, is the design for the pair of cottages on the estate (Fig. 44). They are odd, to say the least: a primitive arched ground floor, built of stone and pebble, capped by what appears to be a tile roof. As executed, the upper floor was timber and the roof thatched, although today the roof is again tiled.

From 1906-1907 Prior built, with A. Randall Wells, what has come to be regarded as one of the best churches of the twentieth century, St Andrew, Roker, Co. Durham (Figs. 45, 46). It is certainly highly original and in general feel has much in common with Lethaby's church at Brockhampton.

Prior did very little architectural work after Roker. St Osmund's Parkstone designed in 1916 with Arthur Grove, and largely supervised by him, may best be considered later. There are several drawings extant at the RIBA for Prior's two rather disconcertingly classical schemes — fourteen for the Cambridge Medical Schools of 1904 and six for the Government Medical Schools at Netley, Hampshire, of 1900, but very few for his pioneering Arts and Crafts work, though this may be coincidental. It may be, however, that Prior, believing in close supervision, and having Randall Wells on site at Kelling and Roker, and himself at The Barn, largely did without the quantities of drawings that usually created buildings. This abdication of total control, also practised by Randall Wells at Kempley Church, Gloucestershire, 1903, was unusual, very different from Webb, Voysey or Lutyens, and not sustained by any architect afterwards.

45 Edward Schroeder Prior. Exterior perspective of Church of St Andrew, Roker, Co. Durham, 1905. Pencil and grey wash (325 x 390).

The design for Roker church is highly original: the windows and tower have the generalised appearance of Gothic, but in their details are quite new. All the curves in the tracery are straightened out to become simple diagonals of stone. It was built of rough, local grey stone.

Notes

1. Lutyens letters, RIBA MSS Collection, 1903, 29 August.
2. *Builder*, LVIII, 1890, p. 355.
3. Ian Nairn and Nikolaus Pevsner, *Surrey*, 1971, p. 307.
4. Hermann Muthesius *The English House*, first English edition 1979, p. 39.
5. Hermann Muthesius, *op. cit.*, p. 39.
6. W.R. Lethaby, *Architectural Association Journal*, XXXIII, 1917, July, p. 13.
7. W.R. Lethaby, *op. cit.*
8. *RIBA Journal*, XXIV, 1917, July, pp. 220-221.
9. R. Norman Shaw to Fred White, 19/9/1905, quoted by Andrew Saint in *Richard Norman Shaw*, 1976, p. 274.
10. 'Goodhart-Rendell's Roll Call' in Alastair Service's *Edwardian Architecture and its Origins*, 1975, p. 478.
11. Hermann Muthesius, *op. cit.*, p. 38.
12. Hermann Muthesius, *op. cit.*, p. 38.
13. R. Weir Schultz in a discussion following a paper given on Lethaby by Sir Reginald Blomfield in the *RIBA Journal*, XXXIX, 1932, p. 308.
14. Lethaby [1]. 121 (FS detail of window backs).
15. Quoted by Peter Savage in *Lorimer and the Edinburgh Craft Designers*, 1980, p. 166.
16. Peter Davey, *Arts and Crafts Architecture*, 1980, p. 64.
17. 'The study and practice of Artistic Crafts', an address by W.R. Lethaby to the Birmingham School of Art, 1901.
18. Reginald Blomfield, *Richard Norman Shaw, RA*, 1940, p. 88.
19. *Architectural Review*, IV, 1898, p. 158.
20. Geoffrey Hoare and Geoffrey Pyne *Prior's Barn and Gimson's Coxen*, Seaforth, Little Knowle, Budleigh Salterton, 1978.

46 Edward Schroeder Prior. Interior perspective of Church of St Andrew, Roker, Co. Durham, 1905. Pencil and sepia washes (355 x 320).

The interior is one primitive space. An open timber roof is supported on great transverse arches resting on paired hexagonal columns which form a passageway between them and the walls. The fittings were not executed as shown here. Over the chancel is a ceiling painted as sky by Macdonald Gill in 1927; there is also a stone font designed by Randall Wells, an altar cross by Gimson and a tapestry reredos by Burne-Jones.

47 Sir Ernest George (1839-1922). Design for two houses at Ascot for W.S. Salting, and for East Court, St Lawrence-on-Sea, Isle of Wight, for Sir W. H. Wills, 1889. Sepia pen and wash (470 x 640).

Exhibited at the Royal Academy in 1889, the *Builder* commented on this design 'Brown ink drawings slightly tinted, in the usual artistic style of execution in which the drawings which go by the name of this architectural partnership are got up, and in which the attempt to make new houses look like old ones is most successfully carried out. It may be questioned whether the effect of the actual buildings, in this respect at any rate, comes up to that of the drawing.' Sir Ernest George regularly exhibited his office designs by means of these perspectives at the Royal Academy. They were all in his own hand. He was also a prolific topographical water-colourist, constantly sketching on the Continent.

48 Edwin Lutyens (1869-1944). Design for the BNDC (*Building News* Designing Club): A Village Smithy, 1888. Pen (355 x 565).

The drawing is signed with Lutyens's anonymous competition motto *Simplex et Prudens* and was submitted when he was aged eighteen and had just entered Sir Ernest George's office.

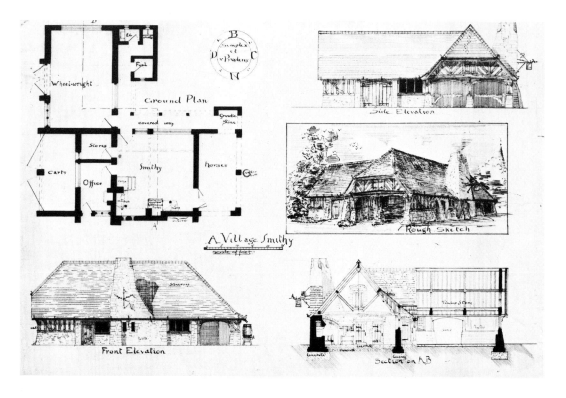

The Office of Sir Ernest George and Peto

Guy Dawber remembered the George office with great affection. 'When I first came into his office, just forty years ago, he was perhaps one of the busiest architects in England, large country houses and other buildings filling his office with work.'[1] George was modest, simple and unassuming and was, apparently, extraordinarily proud of the long list of able architects who had passed through his office. Among them were Herbert Baker, Dawber himself, R. Weir Schultz, Lutyens, Arnold Mitchell, S.D. Adshead, George Drysdale and John B. Gass. Lutyens said in a letter to Lady Emily (his wife) that he had received a letter from George who was going to give them one of his drawings as a wedding present 'saying he always looks upon me as one of his pupils.'[2] Perhaps he had forgotten that Lutyens had left his office after a year, feeling he was wasting his time there.

The office was at No 18 Maddox Street, on the top floor. It consisted of a manager's room, a waiting room, two private rooms, one for George and one for his partner Peto (who was rarely seen for he spent most of his time with clients), and a drawing office for the draughtsmen. There were on average six articled pupils, one or two paid assistants, the manager and various Clerks of Works. George did all the designing himself and it was left to the pupils to trace and to turn sketches into working drawings. Darcy Braddell remembered that George's room was panelled in the Dutch style with oak of the finest quality; there was a little Flemish stained glass in the windows and Italian faience dishes and jars 'to add warm and lovely colour to the beauty of the surroundings'.[3]

George designed in a variety of styles but is best known for his 'Dutch' houses in Harrington and Collingham Gardens, Kensington. For his large country houses he could adopt an Elizabethan manorial style, as at Batsford Park, Gloucestershire, or Stoodleigh Court, Tiverton, Devon, and it was this particular manner of building that was often taken up by Dawber and Lutyens as an Arts and Crafts variant of vernacular. Dawber recalled that George was 'an able and brilliant planner, and the ease with which his buildings grouped together in the particularly picturesque manner he made his own never ceased to excite our keen appreciation.'[4]

It was probably, however, George's own personal style of perspective drawing that had the most influence on his pupils and made his work so popular. He had a soft sepia pen and wash technique that was very different from the ruled black pen and ink perspectives of the Shaw office. It is a soft style well suited to conveying natural textures — tile, brick, oak — and, above all, giving the effect of a building long rooted in the countryside over several hundred years. His approach to design was largely a pictorial one. He did not start by working on a plan or section — but with a brilliant sepia perspective. He also angled his buildings from a low viewpoint, a habit taken up by Lutyens who characteristically called it a 'worm's eye view'. It is interesting, however, to compare George's perspectives with his office working drawings, for example those for Batsford Park (1887) which are in pen and are new and hard in effect, much closer to the buildings as executed.

George, however, could also design in a vernacular style, as his design for East Court shows (Fig. 47). Another influential vernacular design published in the *Studio* in 1897 was his perspective for a cottage in Harpenden, designed in 1888, when Lutyens was still working for him. It was this type of building that proved to be so influential on the younger architects, on

49 Edwin Lutyens. Preliminary design for stables at Crooksbury House, near Farnham, Surrey, for Arthur W. Chapman, 4 April, 1889. Pen and sepia wash (265 x 375).

The 'eye-lid' window, bay and woodwork of the beehive are very similar in detail to Ernest George's work (see figure 47). As executed the stables took a different form and were extended, with cupola, in 1901-1902. The gardener's cottage in the drive was Lutyens's first work as an independent architect, 1889.

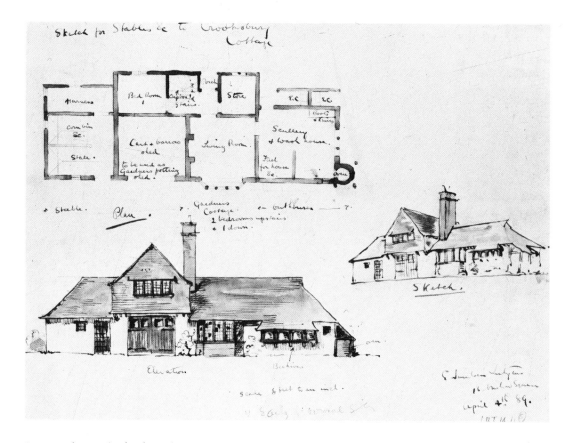

Lutyens in particular but also on Townsend, Halsey Ricardo and Baillie Scott. George published regularly and his work had greater range of scale than Shaw's, providing prototypes for the cottage and the more modest size of house.

Edwin Lutyens (1869-1944) entered the George office in late 1887, at the age of 18, having already spent two years at the South Kensington School of Art. Even at an early age Lutyens was extraordinarily ambitious and frequently entered for competitions. In 1886 he had won an Award of Merit from the *Boy's Own Paper* for a design for a Boys' House of Rest, and in 1888 the National Bronze Medal for a country house, the designs for which are in the RIBA. Then he began to enter for the competitions which were set several times a year by the *Building News* Designing Club. In late 1886 he entered a design for 'A Villa Residence', his scheme being mentioned among the designs which ranked second, and in early 1888 he submitted a design for 'A Village Smithy' (Fig. 48). Again his design, submitted under the motto 'Simplex et Prudens', was placed in the second class, the *Building News* commenting: ' "Simplex et Prudens" draws badly, but has a notion of rural architecture and the advantage of simple lines in such buildings. His plan is, however, as crude as his sketch.'[5] What Lutyens's design does show is his ability to design in a vernacular style in broad, plain masses — particularly evident in the massing of the chimney and deep sweep of the roof.

Being brought up at Thursley in Surrey, Lutyens had a thorough knowledge of local Surrey building techniques. He rambled through the countryside as a boy and spent long sessions in the Thursley carpenter's shop and in Tickner's, the local builder's yard at Godalming. Andrew

Saint quotes the first meeting of Lutyens with Shaw, in about 1888 (the date of 'A Village Smithy'), when Shaw was engaged in alterations to Upper House in Surrey. 'After a little conversation the PRA of the future was telling Norman Shaw RA of his experiments in the Type of building suited to agricultural enterprise; just mud-encased on wooden piles, roofed with heather, resistant to wind and weather, warm in winter, cool in summer, conforming with the surroundings in accordance with what he called "my fixed principles" — this made Shaw smile — and those were, that anything that was put up by man should harmonise with what Nature, who had been there first, should dictate. Materials should be drawn from those obtainable in the area and foreign elements strictly eliminated.'[6]

When Lutyens entered the George office he found the leading assistant was Herbert Baker. Baker remembered that the young Lutyens did little work himself, watching and criticising other people's efforts and seeming to joke his way through his pupilage. It was here that Lutyens began to develop his architectural 'persona'. First came an amused contempt of professionalism which went with a scorn for the futility of sketchbooks; this was no doubt encouraged by the example set by Sir Ernest George who not only sketched constantly but based many of his designs on foreign prototypes. Lutyens and Baker did go on scrambles, the most memorable one being later in 1890 in Wales and Shropshire where they saw Stokesay Castle. Lutyens developed the pose of 'never sketching', but retaining everything in his memory. All his timber work, he said afterwards, was based on Stokesay. There are, however, a set of 54 topographical sketches, datable to 1886-1887, made by Lutyens of vernacular and Gothic buildings in Normandy. In spite of Lutyens's contempt for George's office, he did learn a surprising amount in his short time there.

The most important was an ability to draw. His early designs are badly drawn, a comment made on both his entries to the *Building News* Designing Club. The George office taught him to sketch in perspective, often from a low viewpoint and to compose picturesquely. Lutyens's drawing style — designs presented in ink and sepia wash — was modelled upon George's until about 1896.

In 1889 the commission to design Crooksbury House enabled Lutyens to set up in practice on his own. For the next six years his work consisted in the main of small cottages and houses in the style and materials of old buildings in West Surrey, often executed with details, such as verandahs, bay windows or chimneys derived from the George office.

The sketch design for stables at Crooksbury (Fig. 49) shows his drawing style. This sheet would have been drawn for the client, but has an easy informality. Plan, elevation and thumb-nail perspective are combined on one sheet, a habit peculiar to Lutyens. It is often difficult in his designs to tell if the plan precedes the perspective sketch in invention, or vice-versa. A similar method of presentation is shown in his design of 1894 for the Lodge at Shere Manor, Surrey (Fig. 50).

Lutyens first met Gertrude Jekyll in 1890 at Littleworth Cross where he was building a cottage, now called Squirrel Hill, for Harry Mangles, then the most famous rhododendron grower of his time. Gertrude Jekyll had settled in Munstead in 1877 with her widowed mother, building Munstead House, and in the wood across the road carried out horticultural experiments from 1881. In 1890 she must already have been considering building her own house as her brother, Sir Herbert Jekyll, was bound to inherit Munstead House on her mother's death. Their meeting, accordingly was providential for both of them. Together, Lutyens recalls, they made 'many a voyage of discovery throughout Surrey and Sussex, within a range possible to Bessie and the pony cart she drew. Old houses, farms and cottages were searched for, their modest methods of construction discussed, their inmates and the industries that supported them.'[7] In 1892 Gertrude Jekyll asked Lutyens to design The Hut which was her first small cottage in her wood, built in 1894-1895 as a place where she could entertain her guests. The sketch design for it (Colour plate V), together with an early design for Munstead Wood and sketch for the gardener's cottage, are contained in the so-called 'Munstead Wood Sketchbook' — a delightful and child-like watercolour volume to charm 'Aunt Bumps' (as Ned called her).

Munstead Wood, as executed from 1896-1897 (Fig. 51), is probably Lutyens's finest work in a style based on Surrey vernacular. However, it is no longer an *exact* recreation of Old Surrey architecture, but merely echoes it in materials and general picturesque grouping. The house is large and strictly utilitarian. There is the hall, dining room, large workroom (for Gertrude Jekyll's craft pursuits), study and kitchen quarters. There is no 'Drawing Room', but inglenooks in hall and workroom. It is constructed of Bargate Stone, brick and tile; the massive oak beams of the hall come from local oak trees. The builder was Thomas Underwood (1860-1929) of Dunsfold, (who later built Orchards), the stone mason William Herbert of Witley. The garden elevation (Fig. 51) has echoes of Voysey in its gables; the

50 Edwin Lutyens. Design for the lodge at Shere Manor House, Surrey, for Sir Reginald Bray, 16 January 1894. Brown pen and coloured wash (480 x 510).

Here Lutyens combines an ability to handle local materials — stone, roughcast upper storey, tile and oak with many joinery details such as wooden pegging — with a particularly clever, and unusual, plan for an awkward site. The plan is splayed, with what appears to be a massive chimney at the angle of the splay. In reality the lodge is very small.

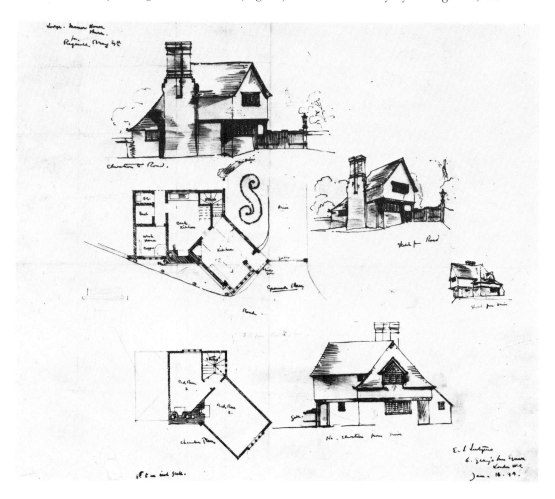

51 George Herbert Kitchin (*c.*1870-1951). Topographical sketch of Lutyens's Munstead Wood, made on the 19 August, 1901, in Sketchbook 9, 1901. Pencil (140 x 230).

Kitchin, who later practised in Winchester, was one of the many young architects who made the pilgrimage to Munstead Wood. Lutyens wrote to his wife, Lady Emily, from Munstead on the 20 April 1901 saying 'Architect Kitchin by name is here — wanting to meet me.'

52 Edwin Lutyens. Design for Deanery Garden (now The Deanery), Sonning, Berkshire, for Edward Hudson, 1899. Pencil, pen and wash (545 x 750). Details, a and b, taken from a larger sheet.

This was Lutyens's first design for a loyal client, Edward Hudson, proprietor of *Country Life*.

entrance elevation recalls H.H. Richardson's work with its round-headed archway, while the kitchen court at the rear is the most antiquarian part of the house with its cobbled yard and timber gallery.

Munstead Wood must always have been very special, a superbly crafted building with a client who believed utterly in 'the thorough and honest spirit of the good work of old days' and who felt that her architect had served her well. It brought Lutyens many jobs in the future, cemented his close relationship with Gertrude Jekyll, and it became a mecca for all Arts and Crafts architects. Many went down to see it and to talk to Gertrude Jekyll. One such was the Scottish architect Robert Lorimer who visited the house in 1897 and recorded the impact of the newly completed house on a young architect in a letter to R.S. Dods in Australia.

> She has bought twenty to thirty acres of a copse across the road, and laid out a complete place there, paths, gardens, bought a barn that was being demolished and reerected it, and some other buildings about the garden, and left a hole in the centre of the ground for the house and now its built . . .It looks so reasonable, so kindly, so perfectly beautiful that you feel that people might have been making love and living and dying there, and dear little children running about for the last — I was going to say, thousand years, anyway six hundred. They've used old tiles which of course helps but the proportion, the way the thing's built (very long coursed rubble with thick joints and no corners) in fact it has been built by the old people of the old materials in the old 'unhurrying' way but at the same time 'sweet to all modern uses' . . . Who do you think did this for her, a young chap called Lutyens, twenty-seven he is, and I've heard him described by the Schultz school as a 'Society' architect. Miss J. has pretty well run him.[8]

The design for Deanery Garden, Sonning (1899-1902), is more suggestive than imitative of the past (Fig. 52). The general impression given is of a Tudor manor house, but the features are sparingly used and free from historical details. Hitchcock calls it 'one of the finest pieces of traditional craftsmanship produced in the twentieth century'[9] and this quality is particularly evident in the plain oak and pegging of the great bay window, the oak flooring and beams inside. The bricks came from the Collier brickworks, Reading.

The drawing has lost its Ernest George styling and is more purposefully naive — something to charm the client, who was, in this case, Edward Hudson, 'dear Huddy', the proprietor of *Country Life.* Lutyens had been introduced to Hudson by Gertrude Jekyll, and he became a loyal friend, not only constantly popularising Lutyens's work in the pages of *Country Life* but also commissioning Lindisfarne Castle and Plumpton Place, and the *Country Life* building itself in Tavistock Street.

After 1900 Lutyens became increasingly interested in classicism — what he called 'the High Game' — and less and less in the vernacular. Lambay Castle of 1905 was his last great vernacular house. But he did retain the language of the craft movement and often used it wherever it was appropriate — for example for garden buildings, as at Abbotswood (Fig. 53), for furniture (the Castle Drogo kitchen furniture, datable to the 1920s), for door and staircase details (constantly), for cottages (as at Ashby St Ledgers, 1907) and for structures such as gates and bridges, as at Plumpton Place (1927).

The design for a well at Mells, 1909, (Fig. 54), is another example of a late Lutyens use of the vernacular. It also shows the office working drawing style, which was strictly utilitarian.

53 Edwin Lutyens. Design for the garden and garden buildings at Abbotswood, Stow-on-the-Wold, Gloucestershire, for Mark Fenwick, 1901. Pen and coloured crayon on tracing paper (760 x 750).

The style of the garden buildings very much follows English sixteenth and seventeenth century examples popularised by Reginald Blomfield's *Formal Garden in England,* 1892, which championed English garden design of before the mid-eighteenth century. The buildings in this design follow the pattern of seventeenth century English gazebos and dovecotes shown in Blomfield. Italianate garden design was considered pretentious.

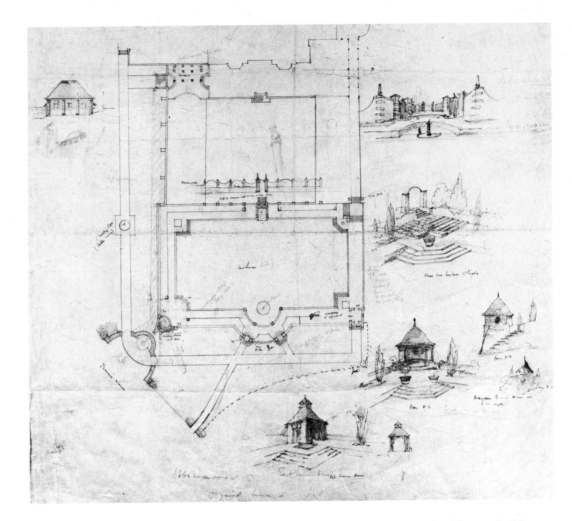

Lutyens believed that drawings were working documents to instruct the builder, and did not like any kind of embellishment. One of his assistants once drew a border around his first drawing in the office, but Lutyens drew a little figure looking round it and said 'What does the builder do with this?'[10] A letter to Lady Emily, dated 5 February 1897, gives a good idea of his attitude to drawings in general:

> I have given my men a warm half-hour here. They ask such stupid questions. I was not cross only very dictatorial and impressive. They never realise that a working drawing is merely a letter to a builder telling him precisely what is required of him — and not a picture wherewith to charm an idiotic client.[11]

Another member of the George office was Robert Weir Schultz (1860-1951), who entered in 1886 and left in the Spring of 1888, just overlapping with Lutyens who came in late 1887. Schultz had spent six years articled to R. Rowand Anderson in Edinburgh but in 1884 came to London, entering Shaw's office where he made many life-long friends, in particular W.R. Lethaby. One hesitates where best to place Schultz, in the Shaw office, or George's —

there are arguments on both sides, but possibly his ability to switch styles and his entrepreneurial skills in dealing with wealthy clients — the Marquess of Bute, Lord Lytton or Mobray Charrington ally him more to Lutyens, Dawber and Baker than to the intellectuals Lethaby and Prior. Although he was a doctrinaire Arts and Crafts man, a vigorous Art Workers' Guild member (from 1891), a lecturer and writer on his favourite theme, 'Reason in Building', he had learnt (possibly from George) to compromise and this led to the success of his practice. He could design in an inflated vernacular style — as at How Green House (1904-1905), or Scalers Hill, Cobham, Kent (1899-1901), but also in 'Wrenaissance' at Pickenham Hall in Norfolk (1902-1905), or gabled Tudor at St Ann's Hospital, Canford Cliffs, Bournemouth (1909-1912). His most 'rational' and free works are the Church of St Michael and All Angels, Woolmer Green, Hertfordshire, and Khartoum Cathedral, Sudan (1906-1913). From 1888-1891 Schultz travelled in Greece, in 1888 with Sydney Barnsley, making a special study of Byzantine architecture and iconography, and wrote a general paper on Byzantine Art for the first volume of the *Architectural Review* in 1897. In 1901 he published, with Barnsley, *The Monastery of Saint Luke of Stiris on Phocis, and the dependant monastery of Saint Nicholas in the Fields, near Skripon,* and later used his knowledge of Byzantine architecture in his work for the Marquess of Bute. Byzantine architecture was much admired by the craft movement, as it had been by Ruskin, for its structural honesty and intricate decoration, and a Byzantine revivalist style was often take up — by Schultz, Lethaby (in detail), Sydney Barnsley at Lower Kingswood Church, Surrey, Henry Wilson, Beresford Pite (see figure 87) and above all by John Francis Bentley at Westminster Cathedral (Fig. 55), which came to represent a model of a 'reasonable' modern building.

Although Schultz worked for Lord Bute constantly from 1891, most of the work was for interior additions and alterations to existing buildings at the House of Falkland and Mount Stuart on the Isle of Bute, or for furniture and fittings. The Scoulag Lodge (Fig. 56) on the Mount Stuart Estate was an exception. Here was a free-standing building, ingeniously planned on an awkward site and demonstrating Schultz's handling of the Scottish vernacular style and local materials. The price was high — £835 — which was £235 higher than the £600 Schultz felt it should cost — but then, as Gavin Stamp has pointed out, it was not a commonplace cottage 'it has a quality which comes more from knowledge and sophistication rather than from that unconscious working within a tradition that the nineteenth century so admired in earlier times.'[12]

There are, unfortunately, no Schultz drawings at the RIBA: the example here is taken from the Mount Stuart archive. This is probably appropriate as Schultz hated the 'professionalism' of the RIBA and never became a member. He too, like Webb, disliked drawing-board architecture and when he retired in 1939 sent many of his drawings away for war salvage, and specified in his will that most of his drawings should be destroyed. He did not believe in 'pretty superficial sketches', and thought that young architects when studying the work of old builders should 'try to get underneath the surface and endeavour to discover their reasons for doing things.' He felt that measured drawings to scale were valuable as historical records and his measured drawings of Greek Byzantine churches, made from 1888-1891, are kept at the Warburg Institute.

His surviving designs are very straightforward and in style of draughtsmanship closest to that of Prior. He never did perspectives, but used different perspective artists to popularise his

54 Edwin Lutyens. Working drawing for a public well at Mells, Somerset, 1909. Pencil (565 x 780).

Designed as a memorial to Mark Horner, son of Lord and Lady Horner of Mells Manor, who died in 1908 while a boy at Eton. The well is constructed of local stone and oak; the carved dedication inside is by Eric Gill.

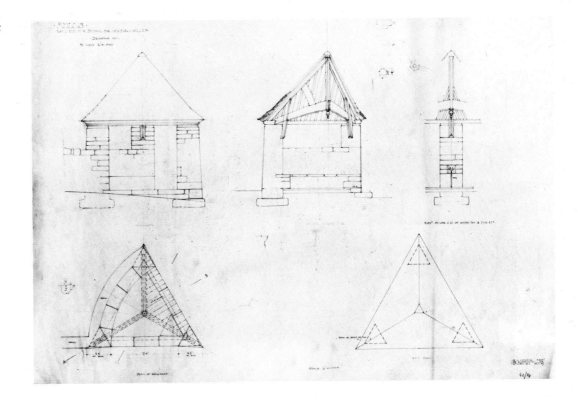

55 John Francis Bentley (1839-1902). Design for the south elevation of Westminster Cathedral, c.1895-1896. Pen and wash (660 x 1220).

Bentley was asked by Cardinal Vaughan in July 1894 to undertake the task of designing the Cathedral. The style was not to be Gothic (to avoid competition with Westminster Abbey) and Bentley records that it 'was thought by the Cardinal that to build the principal Catholic church in England in a style which was absolutely primitive Christian, which was not confined to Italy, England, or to any other nation, but was up to the ninth century spread over many countries, would be the wisest thing to do. Personally, I should have preferred a Gothic church, yet, on consideration I am inclined to think that the Cardinal was right.' The architect went to study the buildings of northern Italy (taking Lethaby's book on *Sancta Sophia* with him) and, returning to England in 1895, he soon had drawings and a huge wooden model (still at the Cathedral) ready, so that the foundation stone was laid in June. The elevation reveals the plan, a model of 'reasonable' building: first the narthex, then the nave of two bays, then the crossing, the sanctuary bay and finally the apsidal choir.

work at the Royal Academy. He did sketch, however, and his sketchbooks and measured drawings are in the possession of Mrs Patricia Keith at The Barn, Phoenix Green, Schultz's house. Other drawings are in the Victoria and Albert Museum, at Mount Stuart, and in the possession of A.B. Waters Esq., formerly Schultz's assistant.

One younger member of the George office, and a remarkable one, was Ethel Mary Charles (1871-1962) who was the first woman to be elected a member of the RIBA. In 1892 she was articled to Sir Ernest George and Peto for three years, and, in 1893 although she and her sister, Bessa Ada, tried to become members of the AA to attend evening classes, they were turned down after a special meeting was held to discuss this threatened invasion of a hitherto exclusively male stronghold. The meeting, incidentally, was convened by George himself, but we do not know whether he supported or opposed the motion!

Ethel Charles, however, undeterred by this failure, passed the RIBA examinations unaided in December 1898, and her sister likewise in 1900. They practised together from a London address, 'York Street Chambers', a block of flats designed by Thackeray Turner specifically to provide accommodation for professional women. Their work was largely in Falmouth, Cornwall, and consisted of designs for houses, cottages, alterations and additions. The schemes, as represented by drawings at the RIBA, are all in a vernacular style and very understated. They show gabled, tile-hung houses with expressed drainpipes and wooden verandahs in the Ernest George manner.

56 Robert Weir Schultz (1860-1951). Design for Scoulag Lodge, Rothesay, Isle of Bute, for the Third Marquess of Bute, 1898. Pen and coloured washes (405 x 530). Mount Stuart Archive.

The lodge was built in the Scottish vernacular style: it was harled, roofed in local green slate, with dressings of Gourock sandstone. Schultz said '— there is always a workable, reasonable, commonsense solution to every problem, and here I would say that it consists in adhering, as near as may be, to the general influence of the type of the district, and not using materials that will jar.' (*Reason in Building*, 1909).

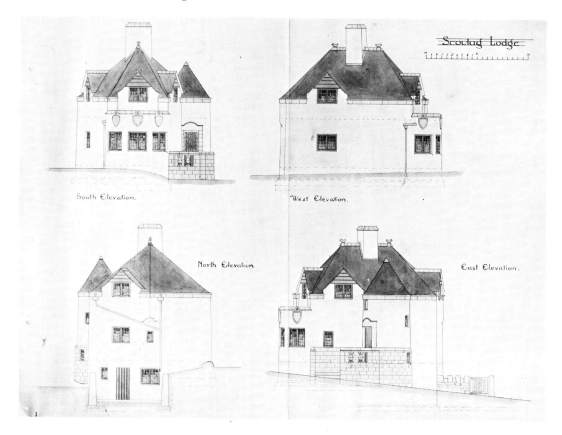

57 Ethel Mary Charles (1871-1962). Design for a block of three labourers' cottages: competition design for the Building News Designing Club, 1895. Pen (355 x 555).

The type of cottage chosen was a Sussex labourer's, with flint walling, red brick quoins, the gables being roughcast.

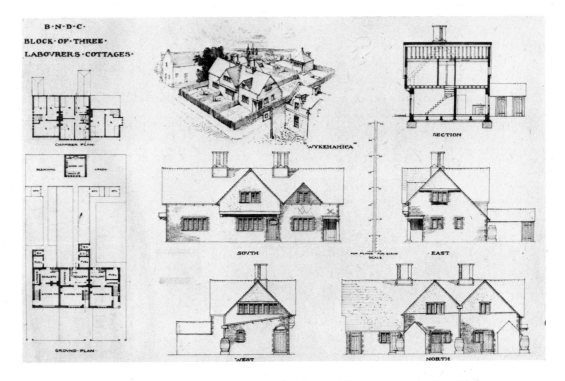

In 1895 Ethel Charles entered two schemes for the *Building News* Designing Club competitions. One was unplaced, but the other, a design for a block of three labourers' cottages, was placed second — a considerable achievement (Fig. 57). The *Building News*, in assessing the designs commented that 'the only true way of arriving at good cottage designs . . was to adopt the vernacular style, to simply depend on the countryside simplicity and hedgerow ideas.' Her design 'exhibits Wickhamica's [her pseudonym] taste and knowledge of cottage architecture and how the old Sussex men used to build under the shadow of the South Downs.'[13]

Notes

1. E. Guy Dawber, 'The Late Sir Ernest George RA', *Builder*, CXXIII, 1922, p. 903.
2. Lutyens letters, 24 May, 1897, RIBA MSS Collection.
3. Darcy Braddell, 'Fugaces Anni', *Builder*, CLXVIII, 1945, p. 6. Also see '"Architects I have known:" The Architectural career of S.D. Adshead', Edited by Alan Powers, *Architectural History*, Vol. 24, 1981, p. 113.
4. E. Guy Dawber, *op. cit.*, p. 903.
5. *Building News*, LIV, 1888, p. 103.
6. Andrew Saint, *R. Norman Shaw*, 1976, p. 310-311, a quotation from Violet Stuart-Wortley's *Grow Old Along With Me*, 1952.
7. Foreword to Francis Jekyll, *Gertrude Jekyll: a memoir*, 1934.
8. Quoted by Peter Savage in *Lorimer and the Edinburgh Craft Designers*, 1980, p. 25.
9. Henry Russell Hitchcock *Modern Architecture*, 1929, p. 87.
10. Margaret Richardson 'The Lutyens Office', *RIBA Journal*, LXXXVIII, 1981, p. 50.
11. Lutyens letters, 5 Feb. 1897, RIBA MSS Collection.
12. Gavin Stamp, *Robert Weir Schultz, Architect, And His Work for the Marquesses of Bute*, 1981, p. 41.
13. *Building News*, LXVIII, 1895, p. 505.

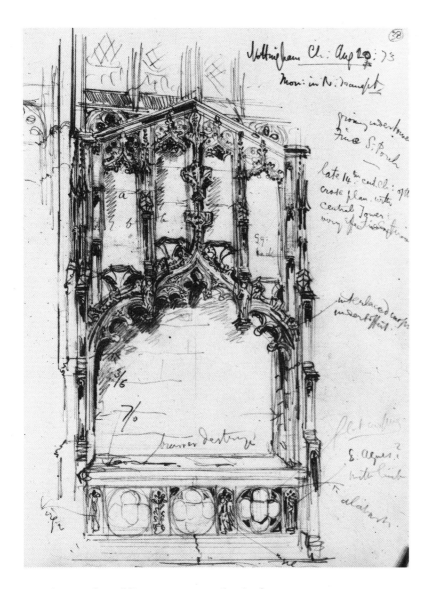

58 John Dando Sedding (1838-1891). Sketch of a monument in the North transept, Church of St Mary, Nottingham, 20 August, 1873, from Sketchbook I, p. 38. Pencil (220 x 175).

The church is almost entirely fifteenth century, with huge Perpendicular windows in the North and South transepts. Pevsner, *Nottinghamshire*, p. 127 notes this monument: 'with niches and mutilated angel figures in the gable, perhaps erected for the Tomb of Thomas Thurland, 1474. In it now an alabaster tomb-chest made probably for John de Tannesley, 1414 and his wife. Quatrefoil panels with shields and small figures of the Annunciation.'

59 John Dando Sedding. Contemporary photograph by architectural photographer Cyril Ellis of the Lady Chapel at Holy Trinity, Sloane Street, Chelsea, *c.* 1900. (RIBA Photographic Collection)

This photograph, in the possession of Arthur Grove who worked on the church, is important as it shows the remarkable gold and brown treatment of the walls, obliterated with white-wash by F.C. Eden in the 1920s. Behind the baldacchino is the gorgeous screen of 1897 designed by Wilson and made by Nelson Dawson.

The Office of J.D. Sedding

The Sedding office was very different from George's as it was characterised by a love of handicraft. It is interesting that the work of Sedding and his pupils — Henry Wilson, Arthur Grove, Ernest Gimson, A.H. Powell, Charles Nicholson and Ernest Barnsley — consistently and exactly realises the theories of the Arts and Crafts Movement. It was the only office to do so. They were what Lorimer called the 'from the roots upwards crew'.[1] Muthesius had a high regard for Sedding's work and said that 'he formed the first bridge between the architects' camp and that of handicraft proper'.[2] He also much admired Sedding's houses, Netley, Hampshire (c.1889) and Flete Lodge (1887) at Holbeton, Devon, and said that they were 'as brilliant as his churches', which is puzzling as both works have a hard Gothic appearance. What is likely is that Muthesius, who cannot have met Sedding, who died in 1891, was infected by his enthusiasms and theories that lived on long after him. His pupils were devoted to him, and his successor, Henry Wilson, wrote a dedicated memorial to his work in 1892.

Sedding's office seems to have been a happy and stimulating place. After the success of St Clement, Boscombe, Sedding moved from 18 Charlotte Street to 447 Oxford Street — next door to the showroom of Morris and Company. The actual amount of his work was small in comparison to other offices, but Wilson recalls 'feverish activity'. He also remembers the 'peculiar half-shy yet eager way in which Sedding rushed into the front room with a smile and a nod of recognition for each of us . . . he would come, and taking possession of our stools would draw with his left arm round us, chatting cheerily and yet erasing, designing vigorously meanwhile.' Or 'if he had been working at any particular drawing the day before he would go straight to the board, throw down the letters half-opened, half-read, and settling on his stool like a bird alighting on a bough would fall to vigorously with pencil and rubber . . . appointments with clients were a grievous infliction.'[3]

John Dando Sedding (1838-1891) had also been a pupil of G.E. Street, and until the mid 1870s worked first in Penzance with his brother Edmund, and then in Bristol, before coming to London. At this time his was a country practice dealing with the restoration of West Country churches: from early on he was interested in local types, and in particular in the English Perpendicular church, as opposed to the early Gothic of France. He found in Perpendicular a freedom of form and naturalism of decoration from which he could create the forms of a modern crafted Gothic. Lethaby said that 'his originality arose in stimulating himself by a study of old work considered not as mere forms, facts, and dates, but as ideas, as humanity, as delight.'[4] Sedding's sketchbooks are filled with very rough studies, always in pencil with many notes added, and mainly of late Decorated and Perpendicular churches in England. The sketch of 1873 of a monument in the Parish Church at Nottingham is a good example of his draughtsmanship (Fig. 58) and of what Lethaby called 'the curious roughness and excited manner of his later sketching style.'[5] His sketchbooks also show him to be particularly interested in carved naturalistic detail.

Sedding had already studied and practised stone carving and ironwork, and in the mid 1870s tried to learn how to draw. In 1876 he met Ruskin and submitted his sketches to him. Ruskin wrote many letters to him, advising, criticising and laying great stress on the necessity of obtaining the texture of surfaces. Wilson quotes a letter from Ruskin to Sedding where he advocates the need for the architect to qualify himself for the practice of his art; 'Modern so-

60 John Dando Sedding. Design for the rood screen, Church of St Mary, Stamford, Lincolnshire, drawn by A.H. Powell, 1891. Watercolour (610 x 405).

The screen, with its flowing and semi-naturalistic foliage, was of a West-Country type; in the cresting are shields bearing the instruments of the Passion, and the rood is flanked by seated figures of the Evangelists. Sedding brought his contractor, Trask & Sons, all the way from Norton-sub-Hamden in Somerset — although there were good local craftsmen in Stamford at the time. Angels painted on the ceiling of the Chancel were the work of Wilson and Edmund Sedding, who were responsible for the drawings, while R. Farrell executed the actual painting. Only the lower part of the screen was carried out; the present rood was erected in 1920 and was designed by a local architect, H. Bailey.

called architects are merely employers of workmen on commission and if you would be a real architect, you must always have either pencil or chisel in your own hand.'[6] Wilson says Sedding never forgot this, and his advocacy for handicrafts, and for the close involvement of the architect in the simple processes of building led him to be a tireless campaigner for the Art Workers' Guild and the craft movement. In the early days before the Guild, Sedding often advocated the theories of the Movement in the pages of the *British Architect*: 'The real architect of a building is something different to the distant dictator who uses the agency of post and telegram to communicate his wishes, who draws the plans, writes the specification and looks in occasionally at the works in progress. He must be his own clerk of works, his own carver, his own director; he must be the familiar spirit of the structure as it rises from the ground, must be ready at hand to meet the passing emergency of site, or crooked wall or awkward chimney . . . and generally to make the most of the site and the building as applied to it.'[7] He himself was at ease with his builders and craftsmen; he employed the same men again and again whenever possible and spent a lot of time in their workshops correcting their carving and ironwork. His decoration was drawn entirely from nature — as his softly drawn cartoon for a fireplace design shows (Colour plate VI). His churches, such as at Holbeton and Ermington, Devon, are particularly characterised by simple carved decoration based on flowers, leaves, animals and birds, a style closely followed by Gimson, Arthur Grove and Charles Nicholson.

Sedding's chuches — St Dyfrig's, Cardiff, and The Holy Redeemer in Clerkenwell established his practice throughout the 1880s, but Holy Trinity, Sloane Street (Fig. 59), came to be seen as 'his perfect treasure house' and was the true exemplar of Horsley's 'unity of art'. Here he succeeded in combining architecture with the work of the best artists and craftsmen. It is well described by Peter Davey: 'Sedding's intention was to create a simple, big, well lit space in which the plain structure dominated and knit together the contributions of individual artists.'[8] It was begun by Sedding in 1888 and finished by Henry Wilson during the 1890s. Craftsmen included Henry Bates (sculptor), Burne-Jones, F.W. Pomeroy (sculptor) and Nelson Dawson (metal worker).

Sedding's practice of combining late Gothic forms with Arts and Crafts detail is often seen in his church fittings, and a good example is his design for the chancel screen at the Church of St Mary, Stamford (1890, Fig. 60), his last exhibited work at the RA in 1891. The perspective was drawn by the architect Alfred Hoare Powell (1865- c. 1960) a pupil of Sedding's, and close friend of Gimson's. Powell's Long Copse, Ewhurst, Surrey, c. 1895, is interesting for its mansard roof and long cranked plan. He acted there as both architect and master of works — all the craftsmen being university men and the building has much of the rustic purity of Prior's work.

When Sedding died tragically and unexpectedly in 1891 Henry Wilson (1864-1934) succeeded to the practice. Wilson had been devoted to Sedding and shared his beliefs, not only in uniting craft with building but that the 'architect should be the invisible inspiring, ever active force animating all the activities necessary for the production of architecture.'[9] He propagated Sedding's ideals constantly during the 1890s particularly in 1892 with the publication of *A Memorial to the late J.D. Sedding*. At first, after 1891 Wilson kept the office together, and with the same team of pupils, completed many of Sedding's schemes — The Holy Redeemer, Clerkenwell, Holy Trinity, Sloane Street and St Peter's, Ealing.

The differences, however, of Wilson's style are immediately apparent; his designs are freer than Sedding's, more original and on a grander scale. His drawings are also more splendid; indeed they are the most dramatically presented of the Movement, and the largest. The draughtsmanship is vigorous, the medium often charcoal and watercolour, or gouache and coloured chalks, often on grey or blue sugar paper, backed, not white cartridge. The perspectives, of course, are drawn to surprise and attract, at exhibitions or for publication, but even the working drawings are vigorously and loosely sketched in charcoal. This illustrates Wilson's theory that drawings should be diagrams, 'skeletons on which the craftsman builds'[10] and not finely executed documents that inhibit the development of the workman's mind.

But by 1895, with only Grove and possibly Cooper remaining in the office, Wilson became more interested in designing jewellery and metalwork, and the collection of designs at the RIBA include designs for crosses, maces, bronze doorways, church fittings, stained glass and war memorials, murals and tombs as well as architectural projects.

Wilson's sense of drama is best shown in his scheme for the extension and redecoration of St Bartholomew's, Brighton, a vast brick church built by Edmund Scott in 1872-1874 (Colour plate VII). Another example of Wilson's Byzantine style is his design for the monument room at Wynyard Park, County Durham (Fig. 61). Wilson's iconography is varied: he draws on Christian and Byzantine symbols as well as classical and mediaeval legend, as can be seen in his design for a clock (Fig. 62).

In about 1890 Arthur Grove (1870-1929) was articled to Sedding, whose brother Edmund

61 Henry Wilson (1834-1934). Design for the redecoration of the monument room at Wynyard Park, Co. Durham, for the sixth Marquis of Londonderry, 1903-1906. Interior perspective showing a tomb chest with recumbent effigy of a soldier beneath a canopy supported on six columns in front of a life-size standing angel holding a basin. Charcoal, coloured chalk and watercolour (1000 x 655).

The perspective is an example of Wilson's own personal style of decoration, which is now far removed from Sedding's crafted Gothic with its naturalistic decoration. It is Byzantine in atmosphere and rich in its materials: he uses different streaked marbles contrasted with chequered floors, Ravennaesque columns and capitals. The coved ceiling has Christian Saints composed and arranged as at Ravenna. Wilson redecorated the Chapel at Wynyard Park and added a monument room from 1903-1906.

62 Henry Wilson. Design for a clock. Pencil heightened with gold (530 x 505).

Mercury, dressed as a Mediaeval knight with a female saint, is surrounded by the twelve signs of the Zodiac.

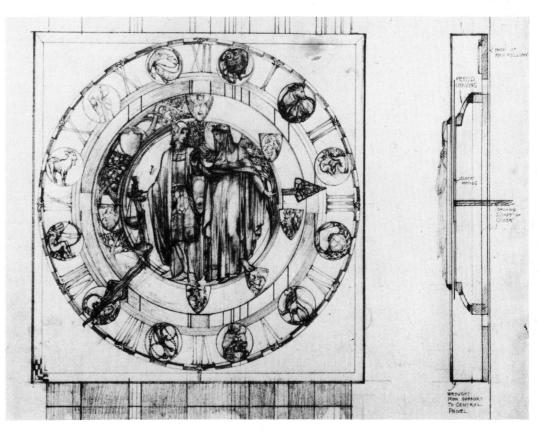

63 Arthur Grove (1870-1929). Design for the chancel, Church of St John the Divine, Richmond, 1905. Pencil and coloured washes (290 x 395).

This is Grove's second scheme, as executed, but differing in details. It shows a mixture of Sedding's Gothic at its simplest with a Wilson-Byzantine veneer in the flooring, pulpit and walling. The first scheme had been very much in the Wilson manner with a Byzantine baldacchino, marble panelling and an elaborate rood. The reredos, chancel murals and stained glass are by N.H.J. Westlake.

(1836-1868) had designed his father's rectory at Govilon, near Abergavenny, in 1867-1868, and after Sedding's death stayed on under Henry Wilson — even though the work in the office was turning increasingly to church fittings and jewellery. In 1904, he set up on his own. One of his first schemes is his design for the chancel, Lady Chapel and vestry at the Church of St John the Divine, Richmond, 1904-1906 (Fig. 63).

In 1906 Grove moved into No. 1 Hare Court, Temple, an office leased by E.S. Prior and sublet to Wilson, Grove and L. Macdonald Gill. Gill (1884-1947), the younger brother of Eric Gill, became assistant to Charles Nicholson and H.C. Corlette in 1903, and after 1906 practised for a time with Grove. But increasingly he turned to graphics, and is best known as a mural painter and cartographer, his picture maps being much used as advertisements and posters. Grove did most of the architectural drawings for his famous Underground map of London, including the accurate plotting of roads. A portfolio of photographs of work by Sedding and Grove, deposited at the RIBA by Grove's son, includes one of a mission church elaborately decorated by Gill (Fig. 64).

Wilson continued to remain part of the group at Hare Court; he had a cottage at Platt in Kent and lived a 'loose life' in London during the week which horrified Mrs Grove. They were all actively involved with the Movement: Wilson and Gill were both members of the Art Workers' Guild, and Wilson its Master in 1917. From 1915-1922 Wilson was President of the Arts and Crafts Exhibition Society and Grove its assistant secretary.

Wilson eventually moved out from Hare Court (retiring to Menton in France in 1922) and Grove moved into his big room. The new third tenant was Harold Nelson who designed the covers of the *Sphere*. Grove's practice was quite prosperous up to 1914 — mostly consisting of church additions in the Sedding manner — but it did not survive the Great War. A late work was the Church of St Osmund, Parkstone at Poole in Dorset, designed with E.S. Prior (Fig. 65). Its generally Byzantine style was determined by G.A.B Livesay's already existing chancel of 1904, but the west front is 'a riot of colour and texture, prophetic of the Expressionism of the twenties'.[11] The brick, mottled from red to brown to yellow, was specially handmade near Wareham. The 57 designs at the RIBA show that Prior did most of the design and Grove the detail. The working drawings are very different from Prior's in that they are brilliantly painted in coloured washes to differentiate materials.

Two members of the Cotswold group were also in the Sedding office in the late 1880s, Ernest Barnsley and Ernest Gimson. The RIBA has no drawings by the Barnsley brothers, Ernest and Sydney, and only one sketchbook and a few miscellaneous designs for furniture and embroideries by Gimson, most of whose drawings are at the Cheltenham Museum and Art Gallery.

Gimson met William Morris after a lecture in Leicester in 1884, and two years later wrote to him asking his advice and perhaps a letter of introduction to a suitable architect in London. At

64 L. MacDonald Gill (1884-1947). Contemporary photograph of the interior of St Luke's Mission Hall, Onslow Dwellings, Pond Place, Chelsea, London, 1910 (RIBA Photographic Collection).

The decoration, which was carried out by Gill and others, was under the supervision of W.R. Lethaby and Halsey Ricardo.

65 E.S. Prior and Arthur Grove. Working drawing for St Osmund, Parkstone, Poole, Dorset. Half-inch detail of dome, *c.* 1913-1916. Print with black and red pen with pencil and coloured washes added (680 x 610).

The concrete proved faulty and the dome was rebuilt in 1922. W. Bainbridge Reynolds designed the lectern, altar cross and candlesticks; Prior the font and stained glass; Eric Gill the inscriptions and MacDonald Gill the grille between the two chapels. Gill sent Grove a postcard in 1920 from Parkstone: 'Here's a view of your splendid church: still a thing of beauty and ever a joy. The mural proceeds but I shan't finish it this time I'm afraid . . .' (RIBA Photographic Collection).

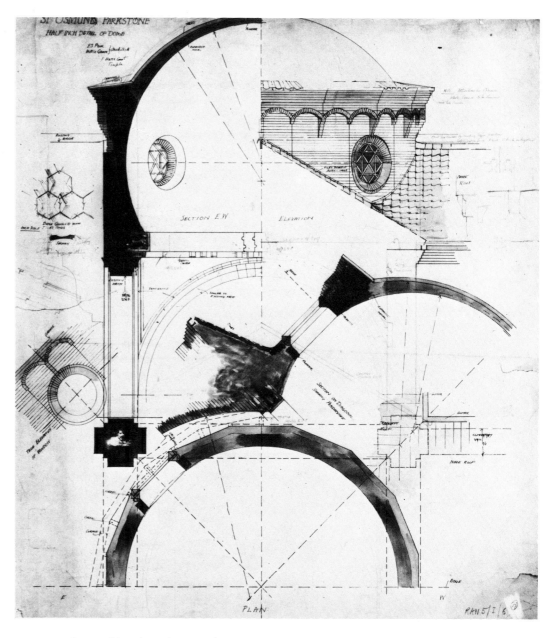

once Morris sent him three letters of introduction, but Gimson only had to present one, to J.D. Sedding, who accepted him at once. Gimson remained articled to Sedding for two years, leaving in 1888 to travel in England and abroad. In 1889, he joined Morris's SPAB, introduced Lethaby to it in 1892, and continued to do survey and restoration work for the Society for the rest of his life. By 1890 Gimson was already learning handicrafts — no doubt inspired by Sedding's teaching. He went to Bosbury in Worcestershire and spent a few weeks working with Philip Clissett, a traditional chair maker, learning the basic techniques of his craft. He also spent a short time with the London firm of plasterworkers, Messrs Whitcombe

66 Ernest William Gimson (1864-1919). Sketches of a kingfisher, thrush, chaffinch and blackbird, from Gimson's Sketchbook, p.10. c.1900-1905. Pencil (255 x 205).

and Priestly, learning the moulding and carving of plaster. Plasterwork, and particularly early sixteenth and seventeenth century English examples of the craft, was one of the interests of the Art Workers' Guild, and many architects of the Movement included the technique in their designs. Gimson, however, was unusual among architects in actually executing his own plasterwork designs. Gimson specified his own approach to the design of plasterwork — the necessity for the worker to 'show in his work something of the pleasure that he takes in natural things . . . and that he should have knowledge of old work so that he should learn from it how to express his ideas.'[12] The RIBA Gimson sketchbook is largely filled with pencil studies of birds and flowers (Fig. 66), all drawn from nature, and are very similar to his plasterwork designs for Borden Wood, Hampshire (1903), Pinbury Park, Gloucestershire (1903) and Wilsford House, Lincolnshire (1905). Gimson also collaborated on his plasterwork and metalwork projects with George Percy Bankart (1866-1929) a specialist in decorative plasterwork, lead and metalwork. A design for wall sconces (Fig. 67) was made in collaboration with Gimson. Hugh Bankart recalled that most of Bankart's drawings disappeared as he rarely (if ever) repeated the same design.

Gimson's architectural output was small in comparison with other architects, probably owing to his preoccupation with furniture-making and to the fact that he had private means. But his few buildings are the most perfect realisation of Arts and Crafts theory. His cottages, and in particular Stoneywell Cottage, Markfield, Leicestershire (1898) and his own house at Sapperton, Leasowes, of 1903, are not simply suggestive of the vernacular, they are vernacular, built from traditional materials with old craft techniques. In the same way Gimson applied vernacular woodworking traditions — for example the constructional stretcher derived from a hay-rake — to furniture design. In this way Gimson, of all the architects, came nearest to fulfilling Morris's hope that it would be from 'necessary unpretentious buildings that the new and genuine architecture will spring, rather than from our experiments in conscious style.'[13] In lieu of an original drawing at the RIBA, the illustration of Gimson's own house, Leasowes, is an engraving by F.L. Griggs (Fig. 68).

Griggs tells a story that Gimson was fond of: 'Once when Ernest Gimson was finishing a house, the builder said to him, "What do I think of it now? Well, sir, in my opinion, it's a great deal too countrified." Annoyed that this was so merrily taken as a compliment, he added "Well, I am thankful to say, our next job is for a real London architect." '[14] Gimson, however, was unable to produce a method of building based on the lessons of the vernacular for more public projects: the exterior of Bedales Library, executed after his death, is in a bland neo-Tudor style, and his Canberra and Port of London competition designs are quasi-Byzantine, rather like Beresford Pite's work. He achieved the interesting distinction of *not* being mentioned by Muthesius.

The true successor, however, to Sedding was Sir Charles Nicholson (1867-1949), who carried his master's crafted Gothic well on into the twentieth century. After Sedding's death, Nicholson stayed with Wilson until 1893, when he set up in practice on his own. From 1895-1916 Nicholson was in partnership with Major Hubert Christian Corlette, and the partnership produced an enormous amount of work which, although it included country houses and alterations to schools and colleges, was mainly ecclesiastical. He restored and refitted many existing parish churches, designed about forty new churches, was consultant architect to six cathedrals — Wells, Lichfield, Portsmouth, Llandaff, Sheffield and Belfast — and Diocesan

Architect to Wakefield, Winchester, Portsmouth and Chelmsford. Goodhart-Rendel, who worked for Nicholson, is almost overwhelming in his praise: 'He was the most remarkable architect who ever lived. He had an extraordinary facility for drawing anything. He designed two cathedrals, Portsmouth and Sheffield and some forty churches. He did not care much for publicity. The number of things he has done without anyone noticing is simply incredible. Also he was violently anti-academic and looked on architecture as an Art. He was in partnership with Major Corlette, but that was an accident and it took Nicholson thirty years to get rid of him.'[15] Or again: 'His choice of forms was, no doubt, largely the result of his antecedents: he was a pupil of Sedding, and heir to Sedding's rich architectural experience . . . he drew boldly and beautifully with a facility that can hardly be imagined by those who have never watched him at work.'[16]

Typical examples of his early church work are designs for a new church, St Matthew's,

67 George Percy Bankart (1866-1929). Design for wall-sconce in pierced metal, made in collaboration with Ernest Gimson. Pencil (260 x 190)

68 Ernest William Gimson. View of the South side of Leasowes, Sapperton, Gloucestershire, engraved by F.L. Griggs in 1922 as the Frontispiece for *Ernest Gimson, His Life and Work,* by W.R. Lethaby, Alfred Powell and F.L. Griggs, 1924.

The walls are of limestone quarried on the site with dressings of Minchinhampton Common stone. The constructional timbers and joinery are of larch and oak grown locally, and the roof is thatched with wheat-straw. The thatcher was John Durham of Fifield, Oxfordshire.

69 Sir Charles Archibald Nicholson (1867-1949). Design for carving, in oak, on the altar for the Church of St Matthew, Cockington, Devon, 1893. FS detail. Pen and wash (270 x 590).

The church was of traditional Devonshire type, with wagon-roof, built of local red stone. The carver was Herbert Read of Exeter.

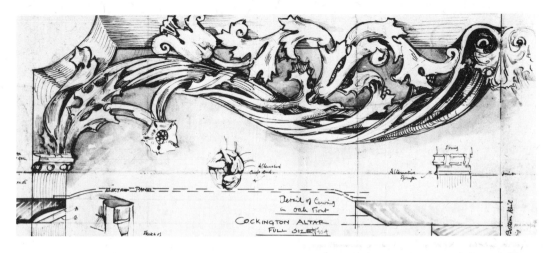

70 Sir Charles Archibald Nicholson. Design for the restoration and refitting of the Church of St John the Baptist, Wonersh, Surrey, 1901. Pen (310 x 270).

Nicholson built the East end of the church in 1901 and designed the screen, choir stalls, clergy desks and font cover. Naturalistic carving on the stalls was by Mr Cushman of Pitsea, Essex, who also worked on Nicholson's St Paul, Halifax, Yorkshire, and St Saviour, Pimlico, London.

Cockington, Devon (Fig. 69) and for the restoration and refitting of St John the Baptist, Wonersh, Surrey (Figs. 70, 71). Both show Nicholson's simple naturalistic carving, derived from Sedding, but maintained throughout his work.

It will perhaps be for the frugal dignity of his low-cost churches that Nicholson will be best remembered. In his own words 'whatever money there is to spend will be used to obtain good internal proportions and not in providing costly ornaments'. His views on the design and arrangement of churches changed little from those expressed in the preface of his *Recent English Ecclesiastical Architecture*, 1911 (with Charles Spooner), where he makes a plea for dignity and simplicity. 'Nothing gives so much unity to an interior as a broad simple ceiling . . . Above all the lesson we have to learn is not to attempt too much . . . When all is said and done, the man who cannot build a cheap church well is not to be trusted to build a costly one.'

An example of Nicholson's brilliant draughtsmanship, a hatched pen hand giving the impression of a woodcut, is his perspective for an extension to St Christopher's Church, Haslemere, Surrey, which was never executed (Fig. 72). St Christopher's is itself a fine Arts and Crafts church of 1902 by Charles Spooner, Nicholson's collaborator. It is free late-Gothic in style and built of Bargate stone with garreted joints and courses of tile set on end — local Surrey materials used by Lutyens at Tigbourne Court in 1898. The interior is a single white wagon-roofed space, with an altar table by A. Romney Green and wall hangings by the Morris firm. Spooner himself was trained in the Blomfield office — in a very different atmosphere.

Notes

1. Peter Savage *Lorimer and the Edinburgh Craft Designers*, 1980, p. 162.
2. Hermann Muthesius *The English House*, p. 37.
3. Henry Wilson *A Memorial to the late J.D. Sedding*, 1892, p. 10.
4. W.R. Lethaby, 'A Note on the Artistic Life and Work of John D. Sedding', *Builder*, LXI, 1891, p. 271.
5. W.R. Lethaby, *op. cit.*, p. 271.
6. Henry Wilson, *op. cit.*, p. 7.
7. J.D. Sedding, 'Architecture: old and new', *British Architect*, XV, 1881, p. 299.
8. Peter Davey, *Arts and Crafts Architecture*, 1980, p. 55.
9. H. Wilson, *Architectural Review*, V, 1898-9, p. 188.
10. H. Wilson, *op. cit.*, p. 184.
11. John Newman and Nikolaus Pevsner, *Dorset*, 1972, p. 334.
12. Quoted by Mary Comino in *Gimson and the Barnsleys*, 1980, p. 48.
13. Quoted by Paul Thompson in *The Work of William Morris*, 1967, p. 56.
14. William Lethaby, Alfred Powell and Frederick Griggs, *Ernest Gimson, His Life and Work*, 1924, p. xx.
15. Nikolaus Pevsner 'Goodhart-Rendel's Roll-Call', in Alastair Service *Edwardian Architecture and its Origins*, 1975, p. 474.
16. H.S. Goodhart-Rendel, *RIBA Journal*, XVI, 1949, p. 290.

71 Sir Charles Archibald Nicholson. Design for panels on the altar, Church of St John the Baptist, Wonersh, Surrey, 1901. FS detail. Pen and wash (710 x 540).

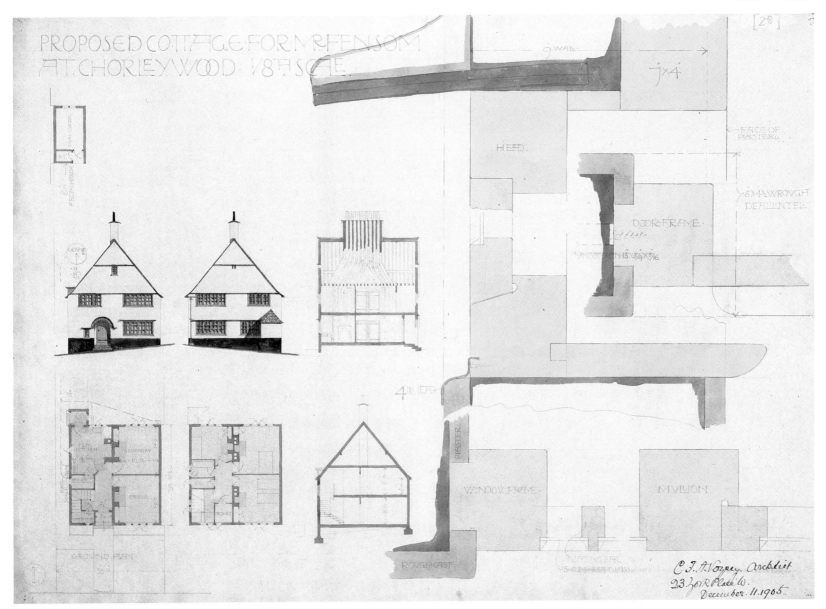

XIII Charles Francis Annesley Voysey.
Unexecuted design for a cottage at Chorleywood,
Hertfordshire, for Mr Fensom, 1905. Pencil and
coloured washes (560 × 780).

This drawing is another example of the way
Voysey included both the designs and working
details on the same sheet. On the left are the
elevations, sections and plans, to ⅛th scale; on
the right are the full-size details of walls,
windows and door frames, coloured pink, yellow
and blue.

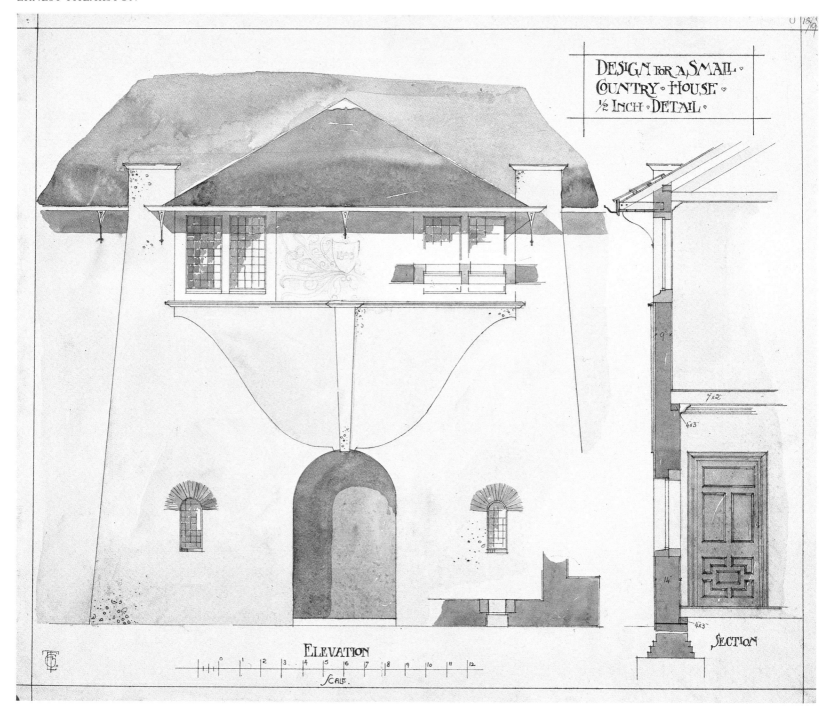

DESIGN FOR A SMALL·
COUNTRY·HOUSE·
½ INCH·DETAIL·

ELEVATION

SECTION

XIV Ernest George Theakston. Detail of the
entrance elevation for a small country house, 1899.
Sepia pen and coloured washes (415 × 490).
See also figure 84.

XV Frederic Charles Eden. Design for a chapel for St John's Home, Cowley, near Oxford, 1901. Pencil and watercolour (485 × 440).

This unexecuted design is unusual among Eden's drawings as being for a completely new building, rather than for church restoration or decorative work. It shows that he could design a simple, almost rural, church structure very much in the Arts and Crafts spirit, combining the rather rarefied Early English motifs — the bell turret, triangular and quatrefoil windows — with rough local stone in an original way. His sensitive watercolour conveys the different colours and textures of the materials he proposes to use. Unfortunately, the design was never executed; the chapel was eventually built by J.N. Comper in 1906.

XVI Charles Robert Ashbee. Design for Nos. 38-39 Cheyne Walk, Chelsea, London, drawn by Fleetwood Charles Varley, 1899. Pencil and watercolour (565 × 425).

Although these houses have been cited as early examples of English Art Nouveau, they were in fact an attempt by Ashbee to recreate the early 18th century style of 'Old London' — houses of the type with brick below and plaster gables above — which he wanted to reestablish in Chelsea. The *Builder* was quick to recognise this and commented on this perspective when it was exhibited at the Royal Academy in 1900: 'A very well executed drawing of a house front in Old London style, brick below and plaster or roughcast above, with all the small-paned windows right up to the face of the wall; the iron railing, decorated with gilt ball finials, is well designed and the whole thing has character, though of a rather archaeological kind.' (*Builder*, LXXVIII, 1900, p. 584). No. 39 was built as a speculation; No. 38, with the tall gable reflecting a studio, was designed for Miss C.L. Christian, an artist. On the immediate right is No. 37, the Magpie and Stump, which Ashbee built in 1894 for his mother and where he had his own architectural office. It was demolished in the 1970s; Nos. 38-39 are now all that remain of Ashbee's work in Chelsea. F.C. Varley, a local Chelsea artist, also painted a frieze in the hall of No. 39 which showed all the buildings along Cheyne Walk from No. 1 to World's End.

38–39 CHEYNE WALK
CHELSEA : S.W.

C.R. ASHBEE · M.A · ARCHITECT.
MAGPIE & STUMP HOUSE:
37 CHEYNE WALK · CHELSEA.

FCV.

Nº 8 ADDISON ROAD W:
GARDEN FRONT
HALSEY RICARDO · ARCHT

XVII Halsey Ralph Ricardo. Design for No. 8 Addison Road, Kensington, London, for Sir Ernest Debenham, drawn by Thomas Hamilton Crawford, 1907. Pencil and watercolour (245 × 255).

This design for Ernest Debenham of Debenham and Freebody's department store shows Ricardo's twin interests — the use of imperishable and washable materials and the architectonic use of colour. Whereas the materials and applied decoration, both inside and out, are by Ricardo's fellow members of the Art Workers' Guild, the architecture of the house itself is classical, drawing from Florentine prototypes, just as Lutyens turned to Sanmicheli for Heathcote, Ilkely, at the same date. The basement, forming a podium, is faced with blue-grey, semi-vitrified bricks. The ground and first floors are enclosed within a giant Florentine motif of pilasters carrying entablatures from which arches spring. These pilasters, arches and cornices are of cream Doulton glazed terracotta and they enclose panels of green and bright blue glazed Burmantoft bricks. The roof is covered with green tiles imported from Spain. The colour reflects the patterns of nature, green being used in the lower elevations to extend the green of the lawn and blue to tone with the sky. Inside the central domed hall, passages and stairs are lined with De Morgan tiles and mosaics by Gaetano Meo. The carving was by W. Aumonier; plaster ceilings in the main rooms were designed by Ernest Gimson and the stained glass was by Prior. The builders were George Trollope & Sons with Colls & Sons.

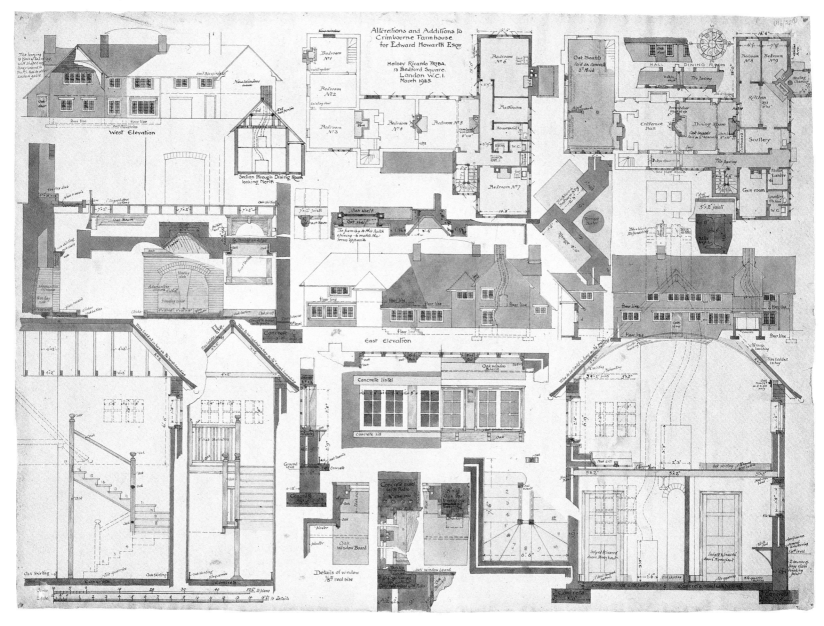

XVIII Halsey Ralph Ricardo. Working drawing for additions and alterations to Crimbourne Farm, Kirdford, Sussex, for Edward Howarth, 1925. Pen and coloured washes (560 × 765).

Ricardo's craftsmanlike approach to his design work is shown here in this closely-packed but clearly organised working drawing. The main plans and elevations are at the top of the sheet, whereas the sections and details are at the bottom, to a larger scale. He also uses the reverse of the sheet for details of chimneypieces. The quality of materials is high: he uses concrete for floors, lintels and sills but oak throughout for staircase, skirtings, window frames and floorboards. An archaic touch is provided in the instruction for the roof: *Tiles bedded in hay on ¾″ rough boarding*.

XIX Charles Edward Mallows. Design for 'Brackenston', No. 8 Tonbridge Road, Pembury, Kent, for the Rev. R.F.W. Molesworth, drawn by Frederick Landseer Griggs, 1904. Pencil and coloured crayons (260 × 520).

Most of Mallows's domestic work was in Elizabethan or vernacular styles and was often quite large in scale. This design is roughcast and gabled in the Voysey manner, but with Tudor half-timbering between the projecting wings. The soft pencil and crayon perspective by Griggs shows a typical Mallows garden design: a formal layout of yew hedges, terraces, pergolas and rectangular beds, in direct contrast to the naturalness and purposely aged look of the house. Mallows produced many designs for gardens, illustrated T.H. Mawson's *Art and Craft of Garden-Making*, 1900, and wrote his own series of articles on 'Architectural gardening' in the *Studio*, 1908-1910. The house was executed in 1904-1905, essentially as in the above design and with a lodge beside the road, also by Mallows. Since 1969 it has belonged to Tonbridge Rural District Council which has altered and added to the existing house to form offices.

XX William Flockhart. Design for a house near Cambridge, drawn by Oliver Hill, 1908. Pencil, watercolour and applied white paint (425 × 725).

Oliver Hill was in Flockhart's office from 1907-1910, and consequently one must presume that this perspective of 1908 is a pupil's rendering of his master's design — particularly as Flockhart is known to have designed everything himself. His known domestic work, however, is not usually in a free Arts and Crafts style, as in this example, although a high tower and tall chimneys appear in Rosehaugh, Ross-shire (1893-1903). It is not known if this design was ever executed.

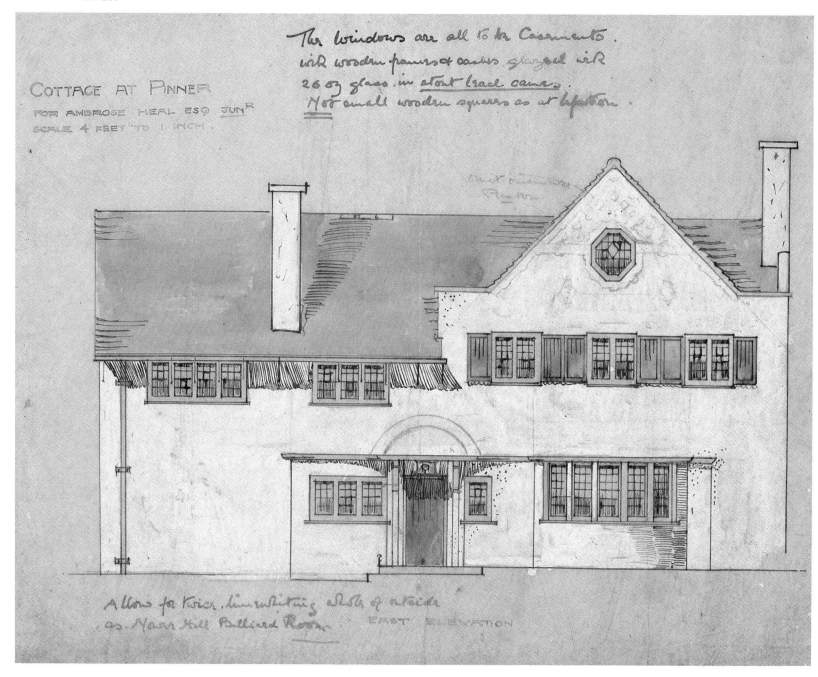

COTTAGE AT PINNER

FOR AMBROSE HEAL ESQ JUN^R

SCALE 4 FEET TO 1 INCH

The windows are all to be Casements. with wooden frames & sashes, glazed with 26 oz glass. in stout lead cames. Not small wooden squares as at hipfattom.

Allow for twice lime-whiting whole of outside as Maur Hill Billiard Room. EAST ELEVATION

XXI Arnold Dunbar Smith and Cecil Claude Brewer. Design for The Fives Court, Pinner, Harrow, Middlesex, for Ambrose Heal Junior, 1900. Pen, pencil and coloured wash on tracing paper (360 × 455).

This house was built for Brewer's cousin, Ambrose (later Sir Ambrose) Heal (1872-1959), the furniture designer. It is a simple and unpretentious version of Voysey's style, with more attention paid to natural colourings and textures than Voysey would have given. It takes its name from a fives court which was incorporated into the garden side of the house between two wings containing coals and the larder at the back of the kitchen block. The Heals must have led a decidedly simple Arts and Crafts life; Ambrose Heal had met Lethaby and Voysey through Brewer and himself collected bill boards and practised calligraphy. They were perhaps like the Honeychurches in Forster's *Room with a View*, living an open-air life, cycling and playing fives.

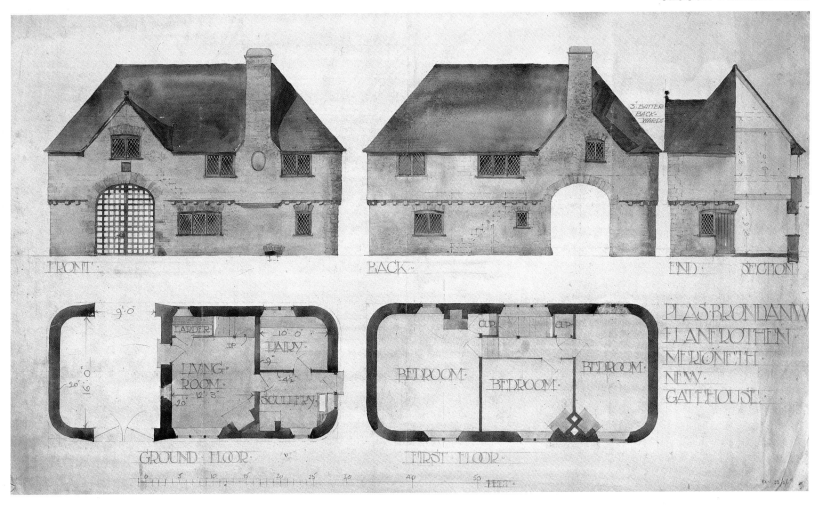

FRONT ·   BACK ·   END · SECTION

GROUND · FLOOR ·   FIRST · FLOOR ·

PLAS·BRONDANW ELANFROTHEN MERIONETH NEW· GATEHOUSE·

XXII Clough Williams-Ellis. Design for the gatehouse, Plas Brondanw, Llanfrothen, Merioneth, 1913-1914. Pencil and coloured washes (460 × 760).

In 1908 Sir Clough inherited the ancestral home of Plas Brondanw, a rambling Carolean 'Plas' set in a wildly romantic estate among the Welsh mountains. It had been neglected and divided into tenements and he put all his energies into restoring the house and gardens. The lodge and orangery were the first two new buildings, built in 1914. The stout lodge, built of rough local stone and roofed in local slate, sits astride the road leading up the Croesor valley to Plas Brondanw. It shows his delight in using the blue, purple and brown local stone: the design with its curved corners and overhang on the first floor shows an almost tactile concern for materials and vernacular form. Sir Clough explains his obsession with the estate in *Architect Errant*, 1971,

p. 93: 'Gradually, yet surely, the old house and its rehabilitation became my chief absorbing interest outside my profession — a passion, an obsession if you like. Yet it was really part of my profession, it was for Brondanw's sake that I worked and stinted, for its sake that I chiefly hoped to prosper. A cheque of ten pounds would come in and I would order yew hedging to that extent, a cheque for twenty and I would pave a further piece of terrace. I had indeed come to reckon all my small earnings in terms of forestry catalogue prices, mason's wages and painter's estimates, and with so many thrilling things waiting to be done how could I find the heart to spend anything but a minimum on mere food and clothing?'

LABOVRER'S COTTAGE·BVRTON COVRT WILLIAMS-ELLIS AND SCOTT ARCHTS ARVNDEL HO. W.C

XXIII Clough Williams-Ellis. Design for a labourer's cottage, Burton Court, Herefordshire, 1908. Sepia pen and watercolour (255 × 265).

Clough Williams-Ellis experimented with many different types of labourer's cottage in the early years of his career. He was a friend of Lawrence Weaver, and this particular cottage was illustrated, with plans, in Weaver's influential 'Country Life' Book of Cottages, 1913. It was a six-roomed, detached type, and rather antiquarian in character, with rectangular plan and lean-to at the rear for coals and a water-closet. There were no passages, so two rooms on both floors could only be reached by passing through others — an arrangement generally avoided by architects at the time. It was not cheap at £240, but did provide a parlour as well as a living room and three bedrooms. The walls were 11 inches thick and hollow, rendered with cement, and the tiles were handmade, so that with its waterbutt and attractive ironwork it had both the style and quality of an older cottage.

72 Sir Charles Archibald Nicholson. Design for the extension of the chancel at the Church of St Christopher, Haslemere, Surrey, c.1914. Pen (390 × 410).

The church was designed by Charles Spooner in 1902 'in harmony with its country surroundings and embodying local characteristics.' The extension was not built.

The Office of Sir Arthur Blomfield

Sir Arthur Blomfield was a Gothic Revival architect much in demand by the clergy of the Church of England for churches, schools and restorations. He was, as his nephew Reginald Blomfield remembers him, 'the most delightful of men, witty and cheerful, a first-rate amateur actor and a skilful painter in watercolours'.[1] He was also 'particularly liked by young men for his genial and companionable manner to them',[2] and was, rather oddly, President of the Westminster Abbey Glee Club. Thomas Hardy had been in Blomfield's office from 1862-1867, and remained friends with him all his life. Hardy used to tell some amusing stories of Blomfield, who was a genuine humorist like his father, the late Bishop of London. Among other strange ways in which he and his pupils, including Hardy, used to get on with their architecture was by singing glees and catches at intervals during office hours. Having always been musically inclined, Hardy could sing at sight with moderate accuracy from notation; hence Blomfield welcomed him in the office choir, where he himself sang the bass. However, the alto part was a difficulty, and Blomfield would say: 'If you meet an alto anywhere in the Strand, Hardy, ask him to come and join us.'[3]

Reginald Blomfield, however, recalls the office in the 1880s almost with disapproval: 'I

73 Reginald Blomfield (1856-1942). Sketch of a red brick and timber cottage, Porchester, Hampshire, from Sketchbook 3, September-December, 1882. Pencil (215 x 260).

During late 1882 Blomfield sketched in Kent, mostly at Tenterden and Aldington, at Radley College and Stanton Harcourt in Oxfordshire — making splendid drawings of the mediaeval kitchen — and at Porchester in Hampshire. His interests are varied; he sketches cottages, manor houses, woodwork, carved ornament, Norman mouldings and forts. His drawing presents the herringbone brickwork and timber frame of the cottage with great clarity.

red brick. cottage. Porchester

74 Reginald Blomfield. Sketch of the corner of a gable of a house in Smarden, Kent, from Sketchbook 2, August-September, 1882. Pencil (135 x 215).

This sketchbook is filled with measured details and vignettes of buildings in Kent and Sussex — details of mouldings, gables, windows, doors, chimneys, brackets and bargeboards. Blomfield's notes show his interest at this time in recording exactly how the buildings were constructed.

entered his office full of enthusiasm, thinking that I should find myself in an atmosphere of high ideals, a modern version of the schools or studios of the Italian Renaissance. Instead of this I found myself in the company of a somewhat depressed managing clerk, two or three assistants and half a dozen cheerful young fellows who were serving their articles as pupils, and most of whom were much more interested in the latest news, sporting or otherwise, than in the latest experiment in Architecture. The usual remark of one of the pupils every morning was "Any spice in the papers?" One pupil, an old Etonian, took a genuine interest in his work; the principal interests of another, also an Etonian, a rowing man and a very good fellow, were shooting and drawing wild ducks, and looking after a lot of boys, the forerunners of the Boy Scouts.' However, Blomfield admitted that 'an intelligent boy who worked could learn a great deal by the study of working drawings in the office, by finishing up and drinking in drawings and by making innumerable tracings required before sun-prints were introduced'.[4] Blomfield and his fellow pupils, amongst whom was Walter Cave, would have learnt all the technical processes of detailing Gothic buildings in Blomfield's office, but for theory or originality they had to look elsewhere. Reginald Blomfield turned to Prior, Lethaby and the Shaw group later on, and Cave and his circle became enthusiastic supporters of the Art Workers' Guild.

Reginald Blomfield (1856-1942) entered his uncle's office in the autumn of 1881; in 1882 he also became a student at the Royal Academy Schools under Phené Spiers, who had been trained at the Ecole des Beaux Arts. Blomfield was a hard worker and very ambitious; at this date his sketchbooks are filled with drawings of English vernacular buildings made on scrambles (Fig. 73). He is a fine draughtsman, possibly the best of the Arts and Crafts Movement, and, never modest, recalled that Phené Spiers wrote to his father in January 1884 saying: 'He is so quick and so hard a worker that I shouldn't be surprised at his making as many drawings in a three month's tour as an average student in a year'.[5] These sketches show Blomfield's interest in the craft movement before his gradual turning to Classicism in the 1890s. In the summer of 1883 he left his uncle and went sketching in France and Italy. On his return he wanted to write a book on Romanesque architecture — preferring it to Gothic for its 'masculine directness' — but instead wrote an article for the *Portfolio* on old Sussex ironwork, a more modest subject. Later, in 1887, he wrote several articles for the *Portfolio* on the half-timber architecture of the Weald of Kent, based on the studies he had made in 1882 (Fig. 74).

In 1884 Blomfield set up in practice on his own and took rooms on the second floor of No. 17 Southampton Street, Bloomsbury. On the first floor was established E.S. Prior, and through him Blomfield met Shaw's men, Lethaby, Macartney, Newton and Horsley and became a member of the Shaw 'Family'. In 1885 he started to attend meetings at the Art Workers' Guild and became a member. From 1889-1892 he was also a member of Kenton & Company, a short-lived Arts and Crafts furniture firm. Blomfield was an enthusiastic supporter of the Movement both at the Art Workers' Guild and at the Arts and Crafts Exhibition Society and must have been a valuable protagonist for his ability to write and speak in a professional manner. His work at this time had definite craft leanings although it was not vernacular in style. One example is the design (at the RIBA) for the hall at his old school, Haileybury College, 1887, which is Neo-Jacobean but with an open timber roof; another is the design for Nos 49-51 Frognal, Hampstead, built for himself and the printer and bookbinder, T.J. Cobden Sanderson in 1892 (Colour plate VIII). Blomfield relates that he was associated with Sanderson in secretarial work for the Arts and Crafts Exhibition Society, and as they both needed houses in 1892 agreed to build a semi-detached pair. 'You want a house', said Cobden-Sanderson, 'Why not buy a site with me and build a semi-detached house on it, one for you and one for me'. He was, apparently, 'a strange creature, highly strung and excitable, liable to sudden violent rages, yet a man of great personal charm when one really knew him. As an artist he was a man of fine taste and a beautiful craftsman in his chosen art of bookbinding.'[6]

The Frognal houses are a good example of Blomfield's work before he developed the 'Grand Manner'. In 1895, Blomfield, who had been the Hon. Secretary of the Art Workers' Guild from 1892, had a row with the Committee and resigned. His book *The Formal Garden in England*, 1892, had been a considerable success and led to many country house commissions: he was prospering and had a lot to do and finally resigned as a Guild member in 1903. Later, in *The Mistress Art*, 1908, Blomfield came to attack Morris, handicrafts and the fundamental principles of the Art Workers' Guild: 'Morris's personal idiosyncrasy and the artistic creed which he had formulated for himself led him to concentrate his attention on the handicrafts, to the neglect of larger considerations of art. The result has been that the sense of proportion between architecture and the crafts has been lost; the architectural sense, the power of putting all these beautiful things together and into their right relation, has disappeared under a prolific growth of cheap accomplishment.'

In the 1880s Sir Arthur Blomfield's practice was almost entirely taken up with church designs. The principal buildings in the office were the Church of the Holy Trinity, Privett, Hampshire (1882), St Alban's English Church, Copenhagen (1885), St George's Church, Cannes (1887), as well as many others. There were also the Fleet Street branch of the Bank of England (1887) and competition designs for the Imperial Institute, South Kensington (1887); these are but isolated examples as it was a very busy practice.

As Thomas Hardy in the 1860s found that architectural drawing in which the actual designing had no great part — as that was done by Blomfield — was monotonous and mechanical, and turned to writing poetry, often giving short talks on poets and poetry to the pupils, so in the 1880s the younger men put their creative energies into meetings at the Art Workers' Guild and into originating such projects as the Quarto Imperial Club.

Nothing is known about the history of the Quarto Imperial Club; its purpose can only be deduced from the contents of two volumes at the RIBA, one of 68 leaves, the other of 64 leaves, both bound in mock vellum. They contain a collection of designs and topographical drawings arranged by subject and executed between 1889 and 1897 by the following artists: Thomas Dinham Atkinson, J.D. Batten, Francis Donkin Bedford, D.C.A. Cave, Walter Frederick Cave, G.C. Horsley, Albert Howell, E.S. Prior, W.B. Reynolds, Frank Cecil Ryde, Charles Spooner, C.F.A. Voysey, E.P. Warren and Gleeson White. It would seem that since some of the drawings carry references to papers read, members met to listen to each others' papers as well as to look at each others' drawings, which were always related to the particular subject of the paper of the evening. In many ways it must have been very close to both the purpose and character of the Art Workers' Guild: the difference being that at the Quarto Imperial Club the subjects discussed were more consistently architectural in theme. Possibly the artists' involvement at the Guild had grown too strong: from 1884 to 1890 there were only seven papers read that were at all related to architecture.[7] The name of the club, 'Quarto Imperial', also had an architectural derivation, since the size of the design sheets was a quarter

75 Walter Frederick Cave (1863-1939). Designs for the interior treatment of domestic windows: at Mouseplat, Sidbury Manor, Devon and at the Nativity church hall, Christmas Common, Watlington, Oxfordshire, October, 1890, for the Quarto Imperial Club, Volume I, p. 44. Sepia pen (350 x 250).

Oak panelling, window seats and decorative plasterwork were features adopted at this time from old cottage dwellings and reused in an inventive way. Mouseplat was a gamekeeper's cottage at Cave's family home; it was widely illustrated in the journals and received some critical acclaim.

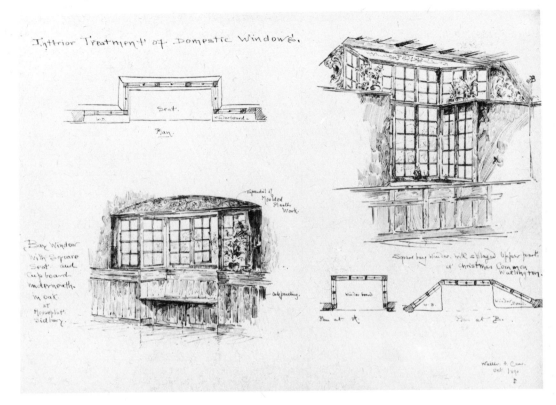

of the size of a standard imperial sheet. The subjects discussed give a good idea of the preoccupations of the Arts and Crafts Movement. Volume I, dating from 1889-1891, contains designs for 'Wrot-iron work' [sic], carving, the external treatment of a town house, the treatment of wall surfaces, cottage architecture, domestic windows, wallpapers, organ cases and towers. Volume II, which dates from 1892-1897, contains designs for furniture, metalwork, outlines (of buildings), staircases, fireplaces, musical instruments and music rooms, screens, the interior treatment of small town houses, bases of statues, book covers, gardens, frames, floors, book-plates and roofs.

It seems very likely that the idea for the Quarto Imperial Club originated in the Blomfield office, as four of its early members, Walter Cave, T.D. Atkinson, F.D. Bedford and Charles Spooner, were all articled pupils in the office in the late 1880s and Walter Cave especially, as has been pointed out, was probably responsible for its formation.[8] He may well have been the Librarian of the Quarto Imperial Club since both volumes appear to have been compiled by him. The lettering on the cover and title page of Volume I strongly resemble Cave's style and the 'QIC' insignia on the title page is repeated only in Cave's own drawings. Almost every drawing in the two volumes is inscribed on its reverse side in his handwriting, and his leadership is underlined by the fact that he delivered the opening lecture which was a paper on 'Wrot-iron work'.

Walter Cave (1863-1939) must have been one of the two 'old Etonians' referred to by Reginald Blomfield as fellow pupils. He was the son of Sir Charles Daniel Cave of Sidbury Manor, Sidmouth, Devon and Edith Harriet, daughter of John Addington Symonds. He was a

76 Francis Donkin Bedford (1864-1964). Design for a chimneypiece, January, 1893, for the Quarto Imperial Club, Volume II, p. 27. Pencil and coloured washes (355 x 255).

Carved in wood and stained green, Bedford's design is more decorative than Cave's (see colour plate IX). It was prepared for the meeting of the Quarto Imperial Club when Voysey read a paper on 'Chimneys and Chimneypieces', and in its imagery of birds and trees coupled with perpendicular forms, it must have complemented his interests. The chimneypiece was considered one of the most important parts of a building at this period. Voysey himself said it was 'the heart of the room — or the countenance of the whole face', and Muthesius noted that 'the fire as the symbol of home is to the Englishman the central idea both of the living-room and of the whole house; the fire-place is the domestic altar before which, daily and hourly, he sacrifices to the household gods' (*The English House*, p. 181).

sportsman; he was in the Eton cricket and football XIs in 1879, 1880 and 1881, and in 1883 played cricket for Gloucestershire. He was articled to Blomfield, and was also an evening student at the Royal Academy Schools, leaving to set up on his own in 1889. He had a large and varied practice which included both urban buildings and country houses. Although he is generally better known for the latter it is interesting to note that he is the architect of the classical but unhackneyed design for Burberry's in the Haymarket (1912). In writing about his houses Muthesius said that like Voysey 'he favours certain characteristics of the "new art", such as tapering uprights and elongated mouldings, closely-set supports for banisters, rough plaster and slate roofs for exteriors. The external appearance of his houses is almost more successful than Voysey's, his surfaces have a broader sweep and the whole is more expressive.'[9] Good Cave houses are Warren Mount (now Robin Hill), Oxshott, and Belgaum, Woking, both in Surrey and dating from the late 1890s. He contributed designs to the Quarto Imperial Club and the two examples reproduced here are typical of his understated drawing style (Fig. 75 and colour plate IX).

Charles Sydney Spooner (1862-1938) is an archetypal architect of the Arts and Crafts Movement. He became Blomfield's pupil in 1885 and also attended classes at the Architectural Association from 1882-1886. He was an architect-craftsman and was known principally for his furniture and ecclesiastical work, church buildings and church furniture. In the course of his long practice, however, he built many small domestic buildings and cottages, which deserve to be fully researched. His best known churches are St Gabriel's, Aldersbrook, Wanstead, Essex (1914), St Christopher's, Haslemere, Surrey (1902) and St Paul's, East Ham, London, his last church and the one he considered his best; he also designed his own house at Burwash, Sussex and war memorials at Hadleigh, Essex and Ranby, Nottinghamshire. He never took a large part in the affairs of the RIBA, of which he was elected a fellow in 1907, but he was a loyal and hard working member of the Society for the Protection of Ancient Buildings, and a member of the Art Workers' Guild from 1887. He ran a furniture school at the Central School of Arts and Crafts with his wife, who was also an artist and craftswoman; he also for a short time started furniture workshops in Hammersmith with Arthur Penty. He often lectured on furniture or 'church fittings' and collaborated with Sir Charles Nicholson in writing *Recent English Ecclesiastical Architecture*, 1912.

Spooner was true to the spirit of the Art Workers' Guild in believing that furniture making was one of the building crafts that made up the art of architecture. He felt that the first things that the maker of furniture should think about were utility, strong and suitable construction and the nature of the material to be used, and that these things applied just as much to building as they did to furniture making.[10] He was a deeply religious man and an ardent mediaevalist; one of his chief aims was 'that the spirit of mediaeval art should be revived, but not the letter'.[11] His buildings were as reticent as his personality: St Christopher's, Haslemere, followed the forms and materials of a late-Gothic country church, even using the local Surrey garreting (small pieces of ironstone inserted in the mortar joints), but yet is unmistakably a modern church of 1902. He contributed twelve designs to the Quarto Imperial Club, and judging by his design for the external treatment of a town house (Colour plate X), was more advanced and progressive in his ideas in 1890 than he proved to be in his later career.

Thomas Dinham Atkinson (1864-1949) and Francis Donkin Bedford (1864-1954) were also in the Blomfield office at the same time as Walter Cave and Charles Spooner, and also

77 Francis Donkin Bedford. Design for the interior decoration of the hall of a town house, April, 1894, for the Quarto Imperial Club, Volume II, p. 39. Pencil and watercolour (355 x 255).

Prepared for a meeting of the Quarto Imperial Club on the 'Interior treatment of small town houses', this design is similar in its unified scheme of decoration, painted freize, light fitting and 'cosy corner' to the interiors of Baillie Scott and Mackintosh. It does, however, surprisingly, pre-date them.

contributed designs to the Quarto Imperial Club. In 1911 Atkinson designed the Solar Physics Observatory in Cambridge but is better known as a church architect and for his numerous publications: *English Architecture*, 1904, *English and Welsh Cathedrals*, 1912 and *Local Style in English Architecture*, 1947. Bedford, although he served his articles with Blomfield, later became a painter and book illustrator and exhibited paintings at the Royal Academy from 1892-1949. He was a member of the Art Workers' Guild from 1901 and served on its committee from 1904-1906 and from 1933-1936. His designs for the Quarto Imperial Club are more decorative than architectural (Fig. 76) but his design for the hall of a town house of 1894 (Fig. 77) is, in its unified decorative scheme, well in advance of any work by Baillie Scott or Mackintosh.

The Blomfield office offered a thorough training in the practical detailing and execution of church buildings. A pupil could become conversant in almost any style as Blomfield had no strong opinions on that subject; he was principally a Gothic Revival architect but could design different versions of Romanesque, or in a classical manner. Blomfield office drawings are clear and ruled in ink, with only occasional washes. They are not artistic, as Street's are, but give the impression of a hard mechanical Gothic. A pupil would also have acquired a thorough knowledge of the materials of old structures, as Blomfield had four cathedrals under his care at various times: Salisbury, Canterbury, Lincoln and Chichester. Spooner and Atkinson certainly continued this ecclesiastical bent in their own work. But there was another side to the office. Blomfield was not dogmatic and a degree of intellectual freedom seems to have flourished there. In his church work he admitted the possibility of individuality in ecclesiastical art, and held that 'where convenience is at stake we ought not to be too much confined by the precedent of mediaeval architecture'. In the matter of materials he did not consider that architects need be afraid of the use of iron, and used iron columns himself in St Paul's, Haggerston and St Mark's, Marylebone. [12] Such progressiveness belonged more to the spirit of the 1860s than to the Arts and Crafts Movement, but at the same time provided a liberal and congenial background for newer and more radical ideas.

Notes

1. Sir Reginald Blomfield, *Memoirs of an Architect*, 1932, p.35.
2. Obituary, The *Builder*, LXXVII, 1899, p.407.
3. Florence Emily Hardy, *The Life of Thomas Hardy, 1840-1928*, 1962, p.45
4. Sir Reginald Blomfield, *op. cit.*, pp. 35-36.
5. Sir Reginald Blomfield, *op. cit.*, p. 37.
6. Sir Reginald Blomfield, *op. cit.*, p. 74.
7. These were: 'Architecture, from the different Craftsmen's points of view' (1884), 'Terracotta' (1887), 'Plasterwork as applied to Ceiling Decorations' (1887), 'Tiles' (1888), 'Architectural use of Coloured Marbles (1889), 'Staircases' (1889) and 'Doors and Doorways' (1890).
8. Walter Cave's leading role in the Quarto Imperial Club has been pointed out by Colin Baylis.
9. Hermann Muthesius, *The English House*, 1979, pp. 43-44.
10. Charles Spooner 'House and Church Furniture' in *The Arts Connected with Building*, edited by T. Raffles Davison, 1909, pp.155-168.
11. Obituary, *RIBA Journal*, XLVI, 1939, pp.311-312.
12. Basil F.L. Clarke, *Church Builders of the Nineteenth Century*, 1969, reprint of the 1938 edition, p.191.

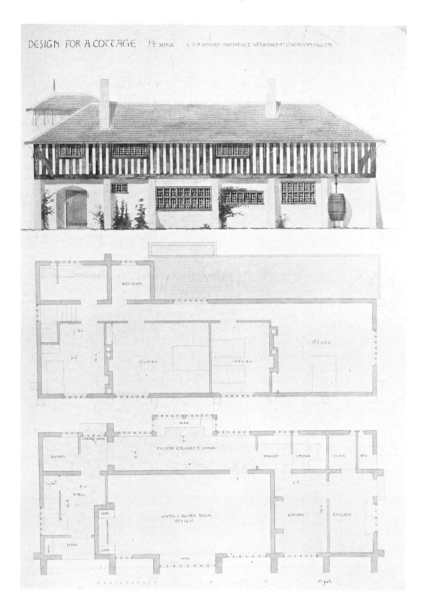

DESIGN FOR A COTTAGE   ¼ SCALE   C.F.A. VOYSEY ARCHITECT 45 TIERNEY ST STREATHAM HILL SW

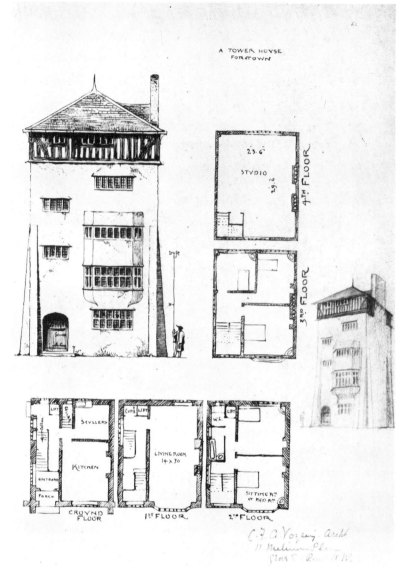

A TOWER HOUSE
FOR A TOWN

This is a modified version of an unexecuted
design which Voysey made in 1885, shortly after
his marriage, for a cottage for himself and his
wife, which was later illustrated in the *Architect,*
XL, 1888, p. 76. The published design was seen
by M.H. Lakin who then commissioned Voysey
to build a similar cottage for a site at Bishop's
Itchington, near Warwick: this proved to be
Voysey's first executed building. The design
makes a definite impact in the pages of the
Architect; it is radically different from its
neighbouring illustration, a picturesque 'Old
English' design for a house at Elstree by
E.J. May. Voysey has taken certain picturesque
features, it is true, probably derived from
Devey's work — the half-timbering, Tudor arch
and waterbutt — but has organised them in a
simple and regular way. The cottage is presented
as a single, two-storey rectangular volume, only
slightly modified by a low square tower at the
rear. He is one of the first English architects to
use the term 'Living & Work Room' for the main
room of the house.

79 Charles Francis Annesley Voysey. Design for
a tower house for a town, *c.*1889, prepared for
the Quarto Imperial Club, Volume I, p. 62,
1891. Pen and pencil with green washes on
tracing paper backed with cartridge (355 x 255).

Although this design was first made in 1889 and
illustrated in the *British Architect,* XXXI, 1889,
p. 70, it was redrawn and re-used by Voysey for a
Quarto Imperial Club meeting on 'Towers' on
the 31 July, 1891. It is interesting as being a
vertical urban design rather than a suburban
one, and as being an early design exercise for the
Forster house at Bedford Park, 1891. Voysey is at
pains to stress that it is a very 'economical' design
and 'might be satisfactorily adapted for a row of
terrace houses'. The plans show that two floors
contain single rooms — the studio on the top
floor and the 'living' room on the first floor, and
that there is a lift as well as two staircases. The
walls have corner buttresses and were to be
roughcast in yellow cement. The external
woodwork was to be painted bright blue, and the
roof to be of green slate, crowned by a spike. The
sheet is particularly interesting as it includes a
rare sketch perspective, and a small figure holding
a measuring rod, which derives from Viollet-le-
Duc's *Dictionnaire raisonné de l'architecture française,*
1854-1868.

Charles Francis Annesley Voysey

Voysey's office, like his architecture, had its own highly individual, almost puritanical
character. Its methodical regime has been well described by John Brandon-Jones,[1] who met
Voysey in the 1930s when he was a pupil in the office of Voysey's son, Charles Cowles Voysey,
whose practice he now continues, and by Noel D. Sheffield, who was articled to Voysey during
the First World War.[2]

The office consisted of two rooms, one opening into the other, for Voysey only had about
two articled pupils at any one time. He never had paid staff. Robert Heywood Haslam (1878-
1954) was Voysey's first pupil and was articled to him in 1895 for three years. His 'Articles of
Clerkship' are in the RIBA Library, which show that an indenture was drawn up between
Voysey and William Haslam, Robert's father, in which it was agreed that, in return for the
yearly sum of £70 Robert would be bound as Clerk or Pupil to Voysey 'to learn the art,
profession and business of an architect and the art of pattern designing' for three years, and
Voysey would 'by the best means in his power teach and instruct the said pupil'. Mr Haslam
had also to agree to maintain his son for the three year period. In 1898, when Robert had
completed his articles, Voysey wrote to his father: 'I cannot speak too highly of Robert's
conscientiousness and diligence and shall ever remember with gratitude his faithful service
during the last three years'.[3]

In all Voysey (1857-1941) had thirty pupils and in his old age compiled a list of their names,
a copy of which is in the RIBA Library.[4] None of them built up practices of note, which may
indicate that Voysey's strict method of office practice inhibited creativity in his pupils.
Certainly Charles Cowles Voysey deliberately decided not to train under his father and
worked instead in the offices of Horace Field and John Burnet. Robert Haslam, for one, had
independent means and never had to live on his architectural work but did things he wanted
to do for people he liked — principally a few houses in the Bournemouth area and wallpapers
in the Voysey style. Tom Muntzer, the son of Voysey's favourite contractor, designed the
extensions to Prior's Field School, Puttenham, Surrey (originally a house by Voysey), but died
in a road accident in 1920, and Cecil Fox who built up a practice on the West coast of Canada
was killed in the First World War.

Noel Sheffield remembers that 'there was no typist, no typewriter, no telephone'.[5] Voysey
designed every building and every detail. He was a marvellously quick and skilled
draughtsman, and also wrote all his letters himself, by hand. It was left to the pupils to trace
the designs, for copies and onto linens for the builder and for planning permission, and to
press-copy the letters (see page 109). There was no design work of any kind for them to do. On
the other hand Voysey went out of his way to teach them the practice of architecture by
actually sitting amongst them in the same room, and by encouraging them to read all the
correspondence and to listen in and learn from conversations between himself and the client
or contractor. Although a very kindly man, he was rather autocratic with his clients and
probably lost work for this reason. He said the only satisfactory client was one who went
abroad whilst the house was building. Voysey's buildings were also not cheap: his construction
was sometimes extravagant, often with waste of material. He had a great dislike of building
restrictions and felt that he should make his own bye-laws.

The office rooms had something of a family character — they were carpeted and hung with watercolours and photographs, and the office furniture was all designed by Voysey. Two drawing cabinets and Voysey's hardwood stool are still in existence.[6] His drawing board was designed to fit his imperial size sheets of Whatman paper, which was square so that he could place his drawings either horizontally or vertically.

Voysey himself had received his training under three architects: J.P. Seddon, Saxon Snell and George Devey. He was articled to Seddon for five years in 1874, who at that time was a prolific Gothic Revival architect of churches, vicarages and schools as well as of the University College of Wales, Aberystwyth, on which Voysey worked. T. Raffles Davison wrote of Seddon's Lambeth Infant Schools in 1881: 'the treatment of the long unbroken street line of the school is a most thorough exemplification of *Power* of design — the power to create variety and charm out of simple material; and perhaps I should add nowadays, the power not to do it in Queen-Anne.'[7] Voysey may have learnt this method of composition from Seddon, and certainly Seddon's old-fashioned devotion to Gothic would have appealed both to Voysey's character and upbringing. Seddon's office drawing style has also much in common with Voysey's. They have the same primitive, but intensely clear, manner of presentation, with a childlike lettering in pencil.

His pupilage completed in 1879, Voysey spent a short time in the office of Saxon Snell, and then in 1880 received an invitation to join the staff of George Devey. From Devey he undoubtedly learnt to incorporate both picturesque half-timbered or Gothic features into his work as well as to use the low art forms of vernacular rural cottage buildings.

Voysey's buildings and theories present many contradictions. He was astonished and embarassed in the 1930s to find himself rediscovered and lauded as a pioneer of 'Modern'

80 Charles Francis Annesley Voysey. Design for a lodge for a Manchester suburb, prepared for the Quarto Imperial Club, Volume I, p. 34, 1890. Pen on tracing paper backed with cartridge (255 x 355).

An overhanging roof shelters and defines the edges of a simple single-storey building. Horizontal bands of windows are placed directly under the eaves which shelter a small verandah with seats in the angles formed by a projecting square bay window. The walls were to be covered in roughcast and the roof with green slates. The design was re-used by Voysey for the Quarto Imperial Club meeting on 'Cottage Architecture' on the 31 July 1890, as it had originally been published in the *British Architect* in March that year (XXXIII, 1890, p. 224).

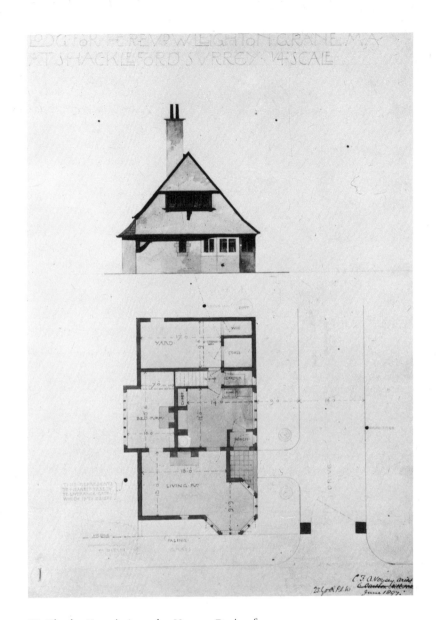

81 Charles Francis Annesley Voysey. Unexecuted design for a house at Colwall, near Malvern, Herefordshire, for C.F.A. Voysey, 1897. Pencil and coloured washes (780 x 560).

Voysey's design for a house for himself at Colwall, a preparatory run for his executed design at the Orchard, Chorley Wood in the following year, is one of his most radically simplified designs. It is a narrow rectangular house with a hipped roof: the uniformity of the front elevation is broken only by the recessed main entrance and by the bay window of the workroom.

82 Charles Francis Annesley Voysey. Design for a lodge at Norney (now Norney Grange), near Shackleford, Surrey, for the Rev. Leighton Grane, 1897. Pencil and coloured washes (780 x 560).

Throughout all his writings Voysey expresses the need, above all, to be simple. This simplicity is often best seen in his smaller buildings, where he was able to collect the rooms under one roof and use the fewest number of features. The plan of this lodge is rectangular with the single conceit of an octagonal corner window; it is comparable in its geometry and composition to Lutyens's lodge at Shere, which was only a few miles away (Fig. 50).

103

architecture. His own leaning was towards Gothic and the two architects he most admired were Pugin and Comper. He disliked the Classical or Renaissance styles, as he regarded these as foreign importations, and Noel Sheffield remembers him as referring to Wren as a 'poor creature', a usual expression of his when he disagreed with someone's views.[8] Yet, although he would not admit it, he was an innovator and was recognised as such in his own day. Lutyens remembered that for him the two surprising events of the 1880s were the work of C.F.A. Voysey and the drawings of Randolph Caldecott. In Voysey's buildings Lutyens saw 'the absence of accepted forms . . . the long, sloping, slate-clad roofs, the white walls clear and clean . . . and old world made new'.[9] Muthesius also saw him as an innovator: 'In both interiors and exteriors he strives for a personal style that shall differ from the styles of the past. His means of expression are of the simplest so that there is always an air of primitivism about his houses'.[10] Although Voysey's practice was comparatively small, his work was much published, particularly in the *Architect*, *British Architect* and in the *Studio*, and in the numerous Arts and Crafts publications on the modern home and cottage; consequently his buildings were influential as can be seen in the early work of a a young architectural student, Ernest George Theakston (see figure 84). He was also an early member of the Art Workers' Guild (elected in 1884, the Guild's first year), exhibited at the Arts and Crafts Exhibition Society and was an active participant in the Quarto Imperial Club.

83 Charles Francis Annesley Voysey. Unexecuted design for a pair of semi-detached cottages at Madresfield Court, near Malvern Link, Worcestershire, for the Earl of Beauchamp, 1901. Pencil and coloured washes (560 x 780).

The principal interest in this design is in the expressive use of a thatched roof. Although unexecuted, the scheme was illustrated in Maurice B. Adams *Modern Cottage Architecture,* 1904.

Voysey's drawings have the same qualities of primitiveness and simplicity as his buildings. They are remarkably uniform; the majority are drawn on imperial sheets of Whatman paper, in an H pencil, with bright coloured washes, or if they are perspectives, full watercolour. The designs are carefully ordered on the sheet, which is labelled in a script designed by Voysey himself. The letters vary in size and in their combination of thick and thin strokes as he felt there was more beauty in variety and change than in what he felt were monotonous block letters. He worked with great speed and seldom used an india rubber; the paper of the finished drawing was as clear as when he started.

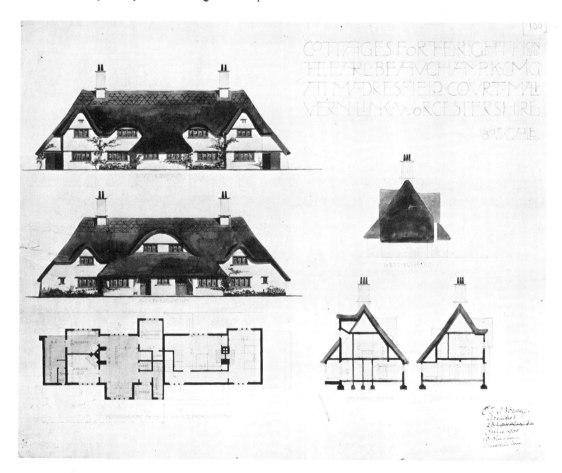

84 Ernest George Theakston (1877-1943). Design for a small country house, 1899. Pen (210 x 310).

Theakston's design was made while he was a student in 1899, either at the South Kensington Schools or at the Architectural Association. The house shows Voysey's influence in its regular forms, white roughcast rendering, buttresses and square chimney stacks, although its design is more decorative than Voysey's. He particularly would not have liked the exaggerated 'Art Nouveau' keystone motif, which he would have considered 'sensuous' and 'distinctly unhealthy and revolting'. (See also Colour plate XIV).

Notes

1. John Brandon-Jones, 'C.F.A. Voysey' in *Victorian Architecture*, (ed. Peter Ferriday), 1963, pp. 276-7.
2. Howard Robertson & Noel D. Sheffield, *RIBA Journal*, XLVIII, 1941, p. 88.
3. Letter to Mr Haslam, RIBA MSS Collection (HAR/1/1/2).
4. They are: R.H. Haslam, 1895; Riley; Tom Muntzer, 1899; R.M.C. Carey, 1900; J.E. Bownass, 1901; E.F.C. Buckley, H.J. Tovey, 1902; C.C. Fox, 1903; A.T. Philips, 1904; Herbert German, 1905; W.J. Burrows, 1906; H.G. Courtney, A. Bailey, 1907; and, with no dates given, W.C. Partridge, F.E. Ravenscroft, Herman Rosse, Stanley Parker, L. Mansfield, L.E. Carreras, C.C. Durston, G.H. Fairtlough, O.O. Harrison, S.E. Knott, N.D. Sheffield, M.E. Stahl, R.G.P. Smith, N.C. Wetherill, F.S. Hulbert, and two women (both for pattern designing), Miss B. Gordon and Mrs Walker. (RIBA MSS Collection) (VOC/1/6 (iii)).
5. Howard Robertson & Noel D. Sheffield, *op. cit.*
6. In John Brandon-Jones's office
7. *British Architect*, XV, 1881, p. 173.
8. Howard Robertson & Noel D. Sheffield, *op. cit.*
9. *Architectural Review*, LXX, 1931, p. 91.
10. Hermann Muthesius, *The English House*, p.42.
11. C.F.A. Voysey, 'Ideas in things' in *The Arts Connected with Building*, (ed. T. Raffles Davison), 1909, p. 120.
12. C.F.A. Voysey, *op. cit.*, p. 124.
13. C.F.A. Voysey, *op. cit.*, p. 123.

In all his writings Voysey repeated his view that 'we cannot be too simple'.[11] The characteristic of his work is his simplification and regularisation of the rural tradition in building. The designs which I have selected from the Voysey Collection at the RIBA for this book (Figs. 78-83 and colour plates XI, XII, XIII) are all based on the forms of picturesque Old English or humble, rural buildings, which have been regularised and ordered into well defined shapes. In 'Ideas in things' Voysey explained how he would build a house: 'So you will gather your flues together, and collect the rooms in such sequence that will enable you to cover them with one roof, or as few roofs as possible. Varying planes at varying angles catch and cut up the lights and shades and add to complexity, to the utter destruction of repose and breadth'.[12] He wanted his buildings to 'play into the hands of nature',[13] and yet, paradoxically, a Voysey house or cottage, especially if it has been freshly rendered, stands out in the countryside as a highly stylish 'modern' work of architecture. In their own day the majority of his buildings were rendered in yellow roughcast and had bright green paintwork, green slate roofs and black, tarred plinths.

Voysey did not make as many drawings for a building as did his contemporaries. There are at the RIBA 75 surviving designs by Philip Webb for Standen (1891-1894) and further drawings at the house, and 229 sheets by Lethaby for Avon Tyrrell (1891-1893). In contrast the largest number of surviving designs in the collection for a Voysey house are the 26 sheets for Greyfriars, Puttenham. This must partly be due to the size of the house, for Greyfriars is much smaller than both Standen and Avon Tyrrell, but it must also be due to two other factors. First was Voysey's use of standard details, which could be re-used for many of his schemes, and second was his economical, almost puritanical habit of conveying his designs and instructions on as few sheets as possible. To do this he combined designs and working details on the same sheet, using colour washes to make the details stand out with clarity.

85 Arthur Beresford Pite (1861-1934). Competition design for a village school, for the British Architect Art Club, 1882. Pen (490 x 630).

This competition design shows Pite's strong and freely-hatched drawing style which won him the RIBA's Soane Medallion prize for his design for a West-End Club House in the same year. He was not so lucky with this entry: his design was unplaced but singled out for its oddity and faults by E.W. Godwin as 'having nothing whatever to do with comparisons . . . whether our comic friend intends me to take his work seriously, or whether he wishes to have his little satirical joke, and by these drawings endeavour to express that kind of picturesqueness that belongs to broken lines, irregularity, and general decay, matters little . . .' (*British Architect,* XVII, 1882, p. 199). Possibly Godwin was offended by Pite's irreverent lettering on the second sheet, *Design for Village School & Schoolmarm's house,* but did he guess that the pseudonym, 'Chichevache', was an old Chaucerian word for 'ugly mug'? Pite's design is, however, progressive for its date and interesting for its cranked plan and free handling of forms and local materials. The strong buttresses dominating the end elevation are characteristic of his work and were later used at his Christ Church church hall, Brixton, and at Kampala Cathedral, Uganda.

86 Arthur Beresford Pite. Design for a house at Temple Ewell, Kent, for C.H. Mowll, 1888. Pen on linen (345 x 510).

In this design made for a relative (his wife's brother was William A. Mowll, Vicar of Christ Church, Brixton), Pite has produced an odd combination of Queen Anne and vernacular features. It is Queen Anne in its pilasters, quoins, picturesque turret and curved end gable, whereas one part of the north elevation is of local diaper brickwork. It is not known if the house was ever executed.

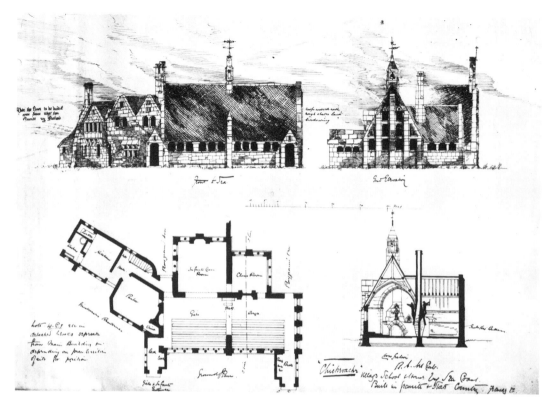

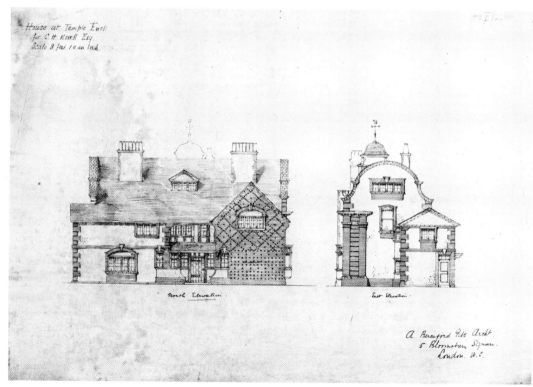

Arthur Beresford Pite, Halsey Ricardo and Charles Harrison Townsend

No comparison is intended between the work of Pite, Ricardo and Townsend. They are grouped together precisely because the work of all three is so individualistic, progressive and the product of no one office style.

Of the three Arthur Beresford Pite (1861-1934) was the least predictable, stylistically. Sir John Summerson said 'he was an individualist, but not in the sense of trying to evolve a personal style. He was interested in everything: Cockerell and the Byzantine, Michelangelo and the modern crafts'.[1] But although he has been principally associated with John Belcher, in whose office he was from 1881-1897, and is mentioned as having some part in the design of the baroque Institute of Chartered Accountants, City of London (1888-1893), and in the Belcher competition design for the Victoria and Albert Museum (1891), he was all his life a pillar of the Art Workers' Guild, of which he was one of the original members in 1884, and a particularly close friend of both W.R. Lethaby and E.S. Prior.

Pite was the son of Alfred Robert Pite and brother of William Alfred Pite. He was articled to his father's firm, Habershon and Pite, from 1876-1881 and worked in the Newport, Monmouth, office as well as later in the London office in Bloomsbury. At this period he also had drawing lessons from William Richardson, from whom he acquired an interest in Dürer's graphic technique, and at this time too developed his own highly personal style of draughtsmanship based on Dürer, William Burges and the mediaeval fantasies of the *Builder* illustrator H.W. Brewer. He always used a Waverley nib and with this could produce a thick, and in reverse, thin line. In the early 1880s Pite was an avid competitor, and particularly chose to enter those set by the British Architect Art Club, which was conducted by E.W. Godwin, from whom he probably developed an early interest in the vernacular. T. Raffles Davison drew a Godwin design for an Irish Cabin in 1881, which he said 'fitted its surroundings of bare hills so perfectly that it might have grown there'.[2] It was Godwin who set the subject for a 'Village School by the Sea Coast to be built in granite and slate', which Pite entered for in 1882 (Fig. 85).

In 1881 he entered John Belcher's office, where he remained until 1897, although he did have an arrangement with Belcher to carry on work on his own account. He set up on his own after this date but did not have a large practice, and no office staff before about 1905. He is best known for his Michelangelesque design for No. 82 Mortimer Street (1893), for Christ Church Brixton (1896-1902, Fig. 87) and for the London, Edinburgh and Glasgow Assurance Company's offices in Euston Square, 1906-1919, his largest London building. He taught architecture at the Royal College of Art from 1900 to 1923, and it is for his work there as a teacher and at the LCC School of Building, Brixton, as Architectural Director from 1905-1928 that Pite in his own day was better known. He was also a controversial and prolific writer and a combative speaker at meetings.

Halsey Ralph Ricardo (1854-1928) also played a prominent part in the Movement as a member of the Art Workers' Guild and as a writer and teacher at the Central School from the mid 1890s to *c.*1910. He advocated the use of washable materials and insisted on the importance of permanent colour as a component of architecture. He was a very original

Notes

1. John Summerson, *The Turn of the Century: Architecture in Britain around 1900,* 1976, p. 22.
2. *British Architect,* XV, 1881, 25 February.
3. Halsey Ricardo 'The Architect's Use of Colour', *RIBA Journal,* III, 1896, p. 366.
4. 'Goodhart-Rendel's Roll Call' in Alastair Service, *Edwardian Architecture and its Origins,* 1975, p. 479.
5. Townsend's life and work has been fully described by Alastair Service, *op. cit.,* pp. 162-182.
6. Hermann Muthesius, *The English House,* p. 41.

87 Arthur Beresford Pite. Design for the side elevation of Christ Church, Brixton, London, *c.*1900. Pen and coloured washes on board (310 x 435).

Designed from 1896-1899 and built in 1901-1902, Christ Church is in Pite's free version of the Byzantine style brought in by R.W. Schultz and J.F. Bentley's Westminster Cathedral (see figure 55). The design shows his interest in layered surfaces to relieve broad areas of brickwork. The exterior facings are of grey, stock bricks relieved with bands of purple Berkhampstead bricks and some Portland stone dressings. The pointing was kept back about half an inch from the face, which increased the textural effect. The bands of purple bricks are varied in number on the different planes of the building, those parts most recessed having more bands than the rest. This is expressed on the drawing by the less structurally important parts having a darker tint. The builder was Mr A.A. Webber of Mortimer Street, London.

designer and thinker and in the 1880s and 1890s produced two of the most progressive designs of the Movement — No. 8 Great George Street, London, 1887 (Fig. 88) and his 1892 competition design for Oxford Town Hall, which took the form of a vast horizontal strip of Elizabethan grid windows between flanking masonry castle keeps.

In all his many writings on colour he made two general points. First, he advocated glazed, imperishable materials and intense colour for the 'streets of manufacturing and crowded towns where there is no other colour', whereas 'in the country the local building materials probably supply us with colour enough to set off and harmonize with the palette served by Nature'.[3] Secondly, he stressed its architectonic use — whereby the architect could dispense with mouldings, cornices and window sills and instead use strong coloured glazed bricks and terracottas to provide a building's form and pattern. It is unfortunate that Ricardo should be chiefly known today for the Debenham house at No. 8 Addison Road, (Colour plate XVII), which although splendid in its use of coloured glazed bricks and tiles, is yet the most overtly classical of all his schemes.

He did, however, have another side to his practice — building many houses in the country in the vernacular idiom. Some, like the Eyot House, Sonning-on-Thames, Berkshire, give the impression of an enlarged village cottage, with hipped-roof and sash windows. Others are more original, particularly his own house, Woodside, at Graffham, near Petworth, Sussex, 1905, which is like a tall mill house, with hipped-roof, sash windows and part roughcast. His design for additions to a Sussex farmhouse shows his precise drawing style and care for local materials (Colour plate XVIII).

Halsey Ricardo is remembered by Goodhart-Rendel, who was his cousin, as being 'dark,

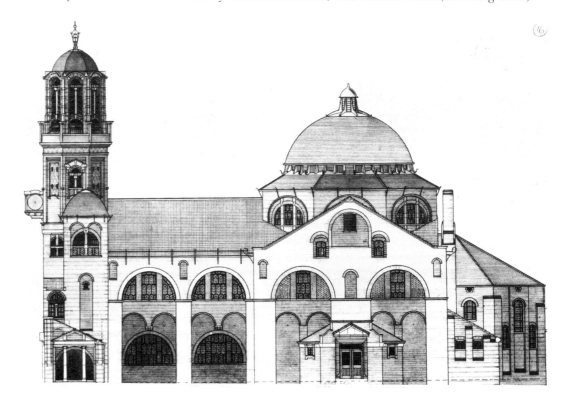

88 Halsey Ralph Ricardo (1854-1928). Design for remodelling No. 8 Great George Street, Westminster, London, for Sir Alexander Meadows Rendel, 1887. Sepia pen (625 x 385).

Rebuilt as offices after a fire, this London building was for many years, until it was demolished in 1928, considered Ricardo's best work. It was certainly remarkably progressive in its assertive use of broad areas of glass in a London facade, and it is doubtful if the design would receive planning permission today. Ricardo himself valued it as being a washable building, his aim being 'to reduce the labour of cleaning and the lodgement of dirt to a minimum'. The walls were built of brown, salt-glazed bricks with bright red rubbers forming the column at the entrance. The woodwork was white and the ironwork gilt. The ornamental trim was in terracotta, by Doulton's. The builder was Mr W. Holt of Croydon. Ricardo was aware of the building's assertiveness and took care to send a vernacular design with it to the Royal Academy in 1888 to tone down its progressive stance.

Jewish, spectacularly good looking and a typical architectural amateur'.[4] He had private means, and no need to train or find commissions, but nonetheless was articled to John Middleton of Cheltenham and then for two years was a pupil of Basil Champney, from whom he learnt a good deal about materials, particularly how to handle red brick. He set up on his own in 1878, and from 1888 he was in partnership for ten years with William De Morgan. He ran his practice from his London home at No. 13 Bedford Square without help from an assistant, secretary or office boy. He often turned down jobs which did not interest him, but lavished much time on those he accepted. He made all his own drawings himself, all of them containing an extraordinary amount of relevant detail clearly packed onto each sheet. He also wrote all his letters himself, by hand, and illustrated them with sketch designs.

In the RIBA MSS Collection is Ricardo's wet copy 'out' letter book, containing facsimile copies of his business correspondence from 1 January 1879 to 25 April 1890. These letter books were often indispensible equipment in architectural offices from the 1870s. A standard book contained up to 1000 numbered pages of tissue paper. Each evening the day's letters would each be placed against a dampened page in the book and interleaved with waterproof oiled paper. The book would be clamped in the press for half a minute and the then letters removed, dried and dispatched. It was a system that enabled architects like Ricardo and Voysey to write their letters by hand, illustrated by sketches, and keep copies, without having to keep a large office staff.

Unlike Halsey Ricardo, Charles Harrison Townsend (1851-1928) is not represented in the RIBA Drawings Collection by his famous London buildings: the Bishopsgate Institute (1892-1893), the Whitechapel Art Gallery (1899-1901) and the Horniman Museum (1896-1901). In these works Townsend succeeded in inventing a new architectural style that has echoes of the Romanesque, Henry Wilson and the American architect, H.H. Richardson. He also succeeded in bringing the Arts and Crafts Movement into the city with three buildings that have as much symbolism and civic pride as the Edwardian Baroque could ever achieve at its best.[5]

He is, however, represented by a set of contract designs for his church at Great Warley in Essex (Fig. 91), and by a collection of designs for country houses which were prepared for publication but never printed. These are more or less uniformly rendered, of similar size, and are mounted on grey-green card inscribed with place name and, sometimes, the name of the client. They are all of houses, cottages and lodges and were obviously intended to form a book on Townsend's domestic work. The designs are not so inventive as those for his public buildings but alternate between rambling versions of Surrey vernacular and free, roughcast Arts and Crafts in the style of Baillie Scott or Parker and Unwin (Figs. 90, 92). They largely represent his practice after 1902 when he tended to busy himself with fringe activities and small commissions. Unlike so many of the architects of the Arts and Crafts Movement, Townsend could not bring himself to adopt the classical style and consequently never received a large commission after 1902. He was a loyal member of the Art Workers' Guild, becoming a member in 1888 and master in 1903, and remains one of the most important architects of the Movement. Muthesius was quick to recognize the importance of his public buildings — 'In this field he is undoubtedly the architect who has achieved the finest results in the endeavour to find a characteristic style based on a personal vocabulary of forms'.[6]

89 Charles Harrison Townsend (1851-1928). Design for Dickhurst, Haslemere, Surrey, for J.H. (or E.H.) Baker, c.1894-1895. Ground floor plan. Pen and blue wash (125 x 240).

Alastair Service has noted that 'its long bent plan is indeed comparable with "skew" plans by Prior, Stokes and others illustrated in the *British Architect* in March and May, 1895 and elsewhere. There was great interest in such elongated plans at the time.' Muthesius found the plan interesting because the hall had ceased to have the quality of a central room out of which all the other rooms in the house open. It had in fact become a separate room with the staircase removed into a picturesque hexagonal tower.

90 Charles Harrison Townsend. Design for Dickhurst, Haslemere, Surrey, for J.H (or E.H.) Baker, c.1894-1895. South elevation. Pen and watercolour (90 x 240).

Townsend had worked for Nesfield and these long elevations show the influence of Nesfield and Shaw's 'Old English' picturesque style, also followed by Lutyens in his Surrey work of the early 1890s. The changes of form and materials (tile-hanging, brick and half-timbering) give the impression of gradual evolution over a long period of time. The contractor is reported as saying 'Mr Townsend should have kept to churches'.

91 Charles Harrison Townsend. Contract design for the Church of St Mary the Virgin, Great Warley, Essex, for Evelyn Heseltine as a memorial to his brother Arthur Heseltine, 1902. Pen and coloured wash (555 x 780).

Great Warley church has roughcast walls, buttresses, a timber belfry, rose window and tiled roofs that tip up at the eaves in a typical Townsend manner. But this simple exterior does not prepare one for the treat the interior provides. There is panelling decorated with lilies and the pointed barrel roof has decorated aluminium bands. The rood screen takes the form of six stiff brass trees, their flowers and leaves intermingling with angels. Most of the ornament is by William Reynolds-Stephens (1852-1943). The building has been seen as one of the three finest church works of the Arts and Crafts Movement, along with Lethaby's Brockhampton and Prior's St Mary Roker.

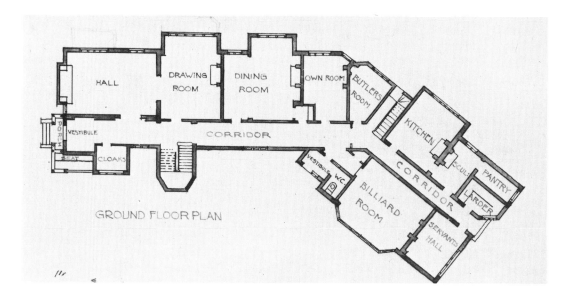

GROUND FLOOR PLAN

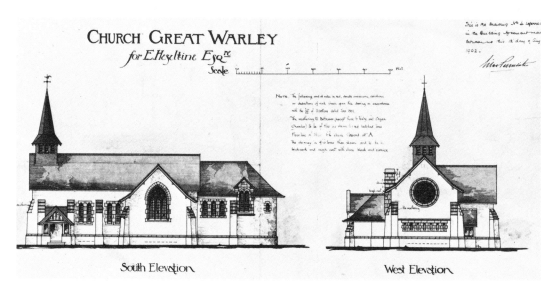

CHURCH GREAT WARLEY
for E.Heseltine Esqre
Scale

South Elevation

West Elevation

92 Charles Harrison Townsend. Design for The Glade, in The Glade, Letchworth, Hertfordshire, for Sir John Gorst, 1906. Pen and watercolour on grey card (360 x 265).

Built in stock bricks, with rough plaster, not roughcast, gabled and with a front door with a circular brick surround and stone hood, The Glade has closer similarities to Barry Parker and Unwin's houses in Letchworth, particularly their own pair of semi-detached houses in Letchworth Lane of 1904, than it does to his own earlier more original designs.

93 Leonard Aloysius Scott Stokes (1858-1925).
Design for the Roman Catholic Church of St
Clare, Arundel Avenue, Sefton Park, Liverpool,
drawn by William Henry Bidlake (1862-1938),
1888. Pen (680 x 510).

The interior of St Clare's is notable for its single
unified space, uninterrupted by piers, transepts,
side chapels or rood screen; it produces its
architectural effect by the opposition of different
planes of surface. Stokes has pierced the wall
piers, which take the form of internal buttresses
in the manner of Albi, to create passage-aisles, a
system derived from Bodley's St Augustine,
Pendlebury, of 1874. The details are also far less
conventionally Gothic: note, for example, the
simply moulded semi-circular arches beneath
the galleries, and Stokes's characteristic mullion-
shaped shaft, which rises from the circular base
of the pier and dies into the cove which carries
the wooden cornice of the roof. The stencilled
decoration of the East end was not executed, nor
were the organ case or reredos in this form. The
interior was unfortunately plastered and is not
ashlar-faced. The perspective was drawn by
W.H. Bidlake who was also in the Bodley office.
He left to set up on his own in 1888 and ran a
successful Arts and Crafts practice in
Birmingham, specializing chiefly in churches.
He was noted at the time for his hatched, pen
draughtsmanship which conveyed the nature of
materials, and which was said to have 'the
breadth and brilliancy of watercolour.' (*Builder,*
LVI, 1889, p. 327).

The Bodley Office

By the 1880s George Frederick Bodley (1827-1907) was the most honoured church-builder in the profession, but did not consider himself to be an 'Arts and Crafts' man — nor was he so considered. He was *not* a member of the Art Workers' Guild, although he did ally himself in 1891 with Shaw and Jackson as one of the group of architects who signed a manifesto against the rise of professionalism published in *The Times*. Nonetheless his office is one of the most important in the Arts and Crafts Movement, both in producing some of its leading architects and for the fact that it was noted not just for its influential church buildings but also for the quality of decoration and handicraft present in those buildings. From as early as 1861 Bodley had acted as a patron of the applied arts when he gave Morris's firm, Morris, Marshall, Faulkner and Company, their first commission for stained glass and painted decoration in his Church of St Michael and All Angels, Brighton (1859-1861). St Michael contains some of the finest early Morris glass, designed by Burne-Jones, Ford Maddox Brown, Philip Webb and Morris himself. From 1869-1898 Bodley was in partnership with Thomas Garner; during the 1870s they produced their two great churches, the Church of the Holy Angels, Hoar Cross, Staffordshire and St Augustine's, Pendelbury, Lancashire. Pevsner notes the contrast between the two: 'it is the decoration one thinks of first when one remembers Hoar Cross. At Pendelbury it is structure.'[1] The two churches had a long lasting influence on Bodley's pupils. Leonard Stokes developed the structural innovations of St Augustine's at St Clare's, Sefton Park, while the luxuriant model of Hoar Cross (as an *English* church in the 'Decorated' manner) was often copied by Sir Ninian Comper, Sir Walter Tapper, F.C. Eden and Edward Warren. In 1874 Bodley, Garner and George Gilbert Scott Junior founded Watts and Company, a firm which still exists, producing wallpapers, needlework, textiles and furniture, much of it designed by Bodley. This did much to increase the reputation of the Bodley office as one that specialised in coloured decoration.

Although Bodley was in his sixties by the 1890s, many of his opinions and methods of office practice had much in common with the more progressive, younger members of the Art Workers' Guild. For example, except occasionally in minor details, he never copied. He had few architectural books and, like Lutyens, was not much of a draughtsman and did not believe in sketching. He had a marvellously accurate and retentive memory, and it was not necessary for him to prompt his memory by making sketches. Edward Warren remembered coming home from a holiday on which he had drawn portions of a church at St Len D'Esserent, near Creil. He showed the drawings to Bodley, who said 'Yes, I remember that church; it had an extraordinary detail like this' and he drew one of the clerestory windows, and various of the details. Warren asked 'How long is it since you were there?' Bodley said 'Let me see; twenty-two years.' 'And he remembered it all. His method was to borrow a chair, take a good cigar, move the chair from place to place and observe the exterior from different points, until the cigar was exhausted, and then he noted the interior and was able ever afterwards to remember all that he saw.'[2]

Bodley, like certain other architects of the Movement — and especially Lutyens, Prior and Gimson — regarded drawing for an architect as solely a means to a definite end, the realisation of his design. Warren remembered that 'for neat and finished drawings he had small regard, and no patience in his later years for their preparation; but his planning was

94 Leonard Aloysius Scott Stokes. Design for the entrance tower of the Convent of All Saints, London Colney, Hertfordshire, *c.*1900. Pen (825 x 475).

Built from 1899-1903, this Anglican convent is one of Stokes's finest buildings. It is a free version of the Elizabethan style, but shows his characteristic 'rational' manner of applying horizontal bands and vertical shafts to a facade. He has incorporated carved decoration into the design: the frieze above the door is by Henry Wilson. It was built of grey and red bricks, with Weldon stone bands and dressings, by Messrs William King and Son of London.

quick and accurate, and his sureness and rapid facility in detail-drawing were astonishing. His little explanatory sketches, rough though they were, were always vividly graphic . . . Of drawing generally, as applied to architecture, he used to say that we all draw too much; and that with one vernacular style, and workmen who understood it, hardly any drawing would be necessary.'[3] Tapper recalled that he loved a 3B pencil and hated needle-pointed compasses.[4] Bodley also disliked accounts and kept none; 'he detested business letters, and frequently delayed answers to important communications — when he answered at all — for weeks or months. If a client became bothersome, he got no answer to any written communication; if he called in a rage, he was received with unruffled courtesy, and generally bowed out smiling and happy in a quarter of an hour.'[5] His pupils remembered him not so much for the practical instruction they received in the office, but for what they learnt from him about the value of handicraft and of colour decoration — for Bodley revelled in the use of paint and gilding upon roofs, walls and woodwork, and for the example he set in his relationships with workmen on the actual buildings: they seemed to have no difficulty in carrying out his ideas.

Leonard Aloysius Stokes (1858-1925) has a prominent place in the Bodley office, but was not a true Bodley pupil as he had been in a number of different offices. In 1874 he was articled to S.J. Nicholl for three years; afterwards he spent a year with James Gandy, a quantity surveyor, and after that worked for G.E. Street, J.P. St Aubyn, T.E. Colcutt and finally came to Bodley and Garner to work on the first competition for Liverpool Cathedral from 1885-1886. His Church of St Clare, Sefton Park, Liverpool (Fig. 93) owed much to Bodley, but Stokes rapidly developed an architectural style along his own lines. H.S. Goodhart-Rendel remembered him as 'a rugged personality with great originality of feeling'.[6] Stokes's church work was basically mediaeval in inspiration, his domestic work was usually derived from English 18th century prototypes, while his other buildings show a free use of both Renaissance and Tudor sources. From 1890 until the First World War he was considered one of the most original architects of the time and received the RIBA Gold Medal in 1919. He played a considerable role in the profession: it was under his presidency of the Architectural Association in 1889-1892 that the association introduced a more methodical system of architectural education with salaried staff and day instruction. He was also President of the RIBA from 1910-1912, and his RIBA presidential portrait, of *c.*1910, painted by Sir William Orpen, shows Stokes in a characteristic pose: a rather scowling figure, standing with clasped hands, in a dressing gown.

Sir Albert Richardson, who was in Stokes's office in 1902, much admired him for the free rationalism of his London Telephone Exchanges — of which the Gerrard Street, Soho, branch was perhaps the finest example (1908, demolished 1936). These buildings were some of the few in the Arts and Crafts Movement to provide a free style for urban buildings. They were characterised by their horizontal and vertical grid facades, with semi-circular windows for the ground storey. Stokes applied the same grid pattern to his more 'collegiate' buildings — for example the Convent of All Saints, London Colney, Hertfordshire (Fig. 94).

Stokes was a devout Catholic and had an impulsive temperament, which was notorious. Richardson remembered that the atmosphere in the Great George Street office was sometimes alarming: 'They started at 9am and had 45 minutes for lunch (17 for the meal and 28 in the Abbey). Stokes sat in an end room making sketches and sending them down to be drawn out. His pupils and assistants ("Damned Colonials" and "Damned Scotsmen" were his two main descriptive labels) frequently felt the whip of his tongue. One day he was swearing at the top of his voice — and the ceiling of his office fell in. He fell on his knees, prayed and crossed himself, gave cheques to all the assistants — and was worse the next morning.'[7]

Richardson only stayed with Stokes for a year, but a far more devoted pupil had been Charles Canning Winmill (1865-1945), who joined the office in 1888 and spent 'four good and happy years with him.'[8] They were both quick-tempered men, but had a great respect for each other. Stokes's name for 'CCW' was 'Purpose-made', for he had some special instruments made for taking certain very accurate measurements. Winmill left Stokes in 1892 to join the Housing Department of the LCC, where one of his first jobs was to work on the Boundary Street Estate; he later also designed many fire stations for the LCC. Through his friendship with William Weir, who was also in the Stokes office and who left to join Philip Webb, Winmill also met Webb, whom he revered; both Winmill and Weir brought Webb's influence to the LCC. Although Winmill had said 'Anything I know of architecture is due to Philip Webb. I partly knew how favoured I was but not wholly.'[9] his early student work, particularly a design for St Thomas's Church Hall, West Ham (Fig. 96) shows Stokes's influence both in its design and drawing style. Winmill's Eton Avenue Fire Brigade Station, Chalk Farm, 1914, also shows this influence in the regular brick shafts of the tower.

Sir Robert Lorimer (1864-1929), the leading Scottish Arts and Crafts architect, spent a short time in the Bodley office in London in 1889-1890. He had been articled to Rowand Anderson and Hew Wardrop in Edinburgh in 1884 and had met Bodley at a conference there in the late 1880s. Lorimer was much attracted by Bodley's Arts and Crafts approach to design and for this reason applied to join his office in London. 'He had to wait for an opening, but filled his spare time with a study of Bodley's work so thorough that he used to boast that when he got there he found that he knew more about the past work of the office than the staff who were already there.'[10] Bodley, however, did not offer much by way of instruction and instead gave his pupils the run of his house with its exquisite fabrics and furnishings. Consequently in 1891

95 Leonard Aloysius Scott Stokes. Topographical drawing of Littleshaw, Camp Road, Woldingham, Surrey, drawn by T. Raffles Davison, 1904. Sepia pen (290 x 470).

Littleshaw was Stokes's own house and was built into a steep hillside. Its freely ranging forms are dictated by the site and by the desire to give the principal rooms the best views over Surrey. On the 'ground' floor, the bay window and long, horizontal strip of windows reflect the dining room and the hall-parlour, which became an open-air verandah in the summer. A skittle alley and heating chamber occupied the lowest level. The house was built of brick and finished with white roughcast, with natural cement coloured dressings round the windows, white woodwork and a red-tiled roof.

LITTLESHAW
South & West Fronts

Lorimer moved to James Maclaren's office and then back to Scotland. He kept up his English connections, however, and particularly admired Lutyens's work. From the mid 1890s he wrote a series of letters to his architect friend R.S. Dods in Australia, keeping him up to date with all the new buildings and current gossip. They form a fascinating glimpse of the architectural world at the time, and particularly of the Arts and Crafts clique. Lorimer had definite reservations about the Art Workers' Guild, and when he heard he had been elected a member in 1897 wrote 'I suppose I ought to be proud to be associated with C.R. Ashbee, Voysey etc'; he also commented on the 'artificial crudeness of the stuff at the A & C' (the Arts and Crafts Exhibition Society).[11]

In the late 1890s Lorimer received a number of commissions outside Scotland; he met Gertrude Jekyll in 1896, and in 1898 designed Whinfold, Hascombe, Surrey, and in 1901 High Barn, Hascombe (Figure 97). Both show his debt to Lutyens and both have Jekyll gardens. A Scottish house, Wayside, at St Andrew's, Fife (1901), shows the influence of Lutyens on his work at home; generally, however, Lorimer's buildings are influenced far more by Scottish vernacular and are more rugged than the work of his English contemporaries.

The true followers of Bodley's practice were the ecclesiastical architects Frederic Charles Eden (1864-1944) and Sir John Ninian Comper (1864-1960), who were particularly constant to the Bodley tradition of designing every aspect of church decoration — stained glass, woodwork and church fitments. Eden was much admired by his contemporaries, and especially by Sir Charles Nicholson, as a leading church architect. He only built, however, one

96 Charles Canning Winmill (1865-1945). Design for St Thomas's Church Hall, West Ham, Essex, 1891. Pen (315 x 415).

This design was made while Winmill was in Stokes's office but was sent for exhibition to the Royal Academy in 1891 as an independent work. It shows the influence of Stokes's work — particularly in its Tudor detailing and the characteristic 'grid' effect of horizontally aligned windows which have their panes divided by vertical mullions. Winmill worked on St Clare's, Sefton Park, and Boxwood Court, Herefordshire, when he first joined the office.

97 Robert Stodart Lorimer (1864-1929). Design for High Barn, Hascombe, Surrey, for the Hon. Stuart Bouverie, 1901. Print (450 x 730).

High Barn is a Lorimer building very much in the style of Lutyens, whose work he greatly admired, and in Lutyens country. By 1898 Lorimer had begun to get a small but regular number of commissions outside Scotland; he met Gertrude Jekyll and visited Munstead Wood and Orchards. High Barn, which has a Jekyll garden, is built of Bargate stone and coursed rubble textured like a Lutyens building. It also has a number of Lutyens features, not all of them visible on this drawing: three double-height bay windows like the studio window at Orchards, and a hanging balcony, on the right, like the one at Tigbourne Court. But there are also several Scottish motifs — not all of them appropriate to the Surrey countryside — in particular the front door with its curved Scottish Jacobean gable and the curved dormers on the kitchen wing on the left.

98 Frederic Charles Eden (1864-1944). Design for the chancel screen, Church of St Lawrence, Combe, Oxfordshire, c.1901. Pen (420 x 655).

Eden modelled his church woodwork on prototypes of the thirteenth and fourteenth centuries found in small country churches in the West of England. His ornament was based on simple, naturalistic carved foliage, and was in oak, or painted. This particular example of a combined screen and rood loft was not executed but many others were — notably screens in the Church of St Protus and St Hyacinth, Blisland, Cornwall, 1896 and in the Church of All Saints, North Cerney, Gloucestershire, 1925.

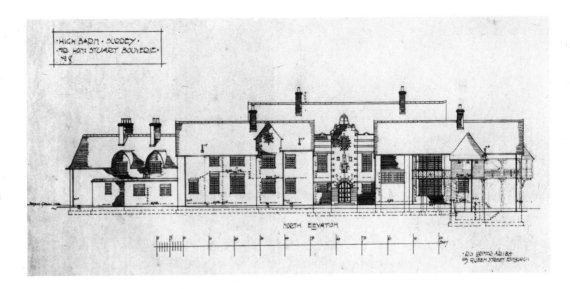

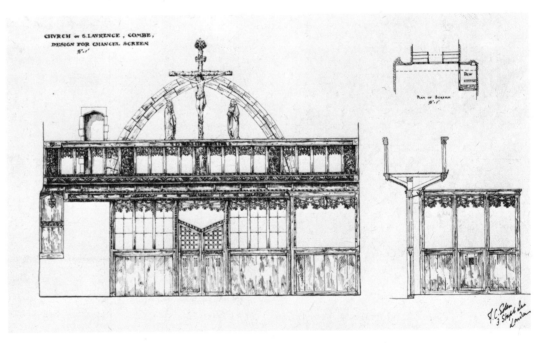

completely new church, St George's, Wash Common, Newbury, Berkshire (1933), which was completed by S.E. Dykes-Bower after Eden's death. What he generally did was to redesign the whole interior of a number of churches with great tact and feeling for materials and detail — either following Bodley's preference for the Early English or Decorated style or using, as at St Mary's, Elham, Kent, a mixture of City Church woodwork and the Florentine Quattrocento. The RIBA has many designs by Eden for church woodwork, embroidery and stained glass, and Eden had his own stained glass works in London in Red Lion Square.

Comper's early church interiors, and especially St Cyprian's, Clarence Gate (Fig. 99) were

99 William Bucknall (1851-1944) and Sir John
Ninian Comper (1864-1960). Design for the
Church of St Cyprian, Clarence Gate, Marylebone,
London, 1902. Pen (520 x 330).

During his early years Comper supported the
'English Use' movement in the Church of England
which wanted, both in its ritual and church
furnishings, to return to the genuine English
tradition of the Middle Ages. The aim of
St Cyprian's was, in Comper's words, 'to fulfil
the ideal of the English Parish Church . . . and to
do so in the last manner of English architecture'
— 'last' meaning English Perpendicular. With its
plain interior and open timber roof, the church
is a reproduction of the East Anglian type of
St Peter Mancroft, Norwich, or St Peter and Paul,
Lavenham, Suffolk. The plain white plaster walls
and arcades of its interior, which is its chief glory,
heightens the preciousness of the richly gilded
screen which stretches across the full width of the
church. When the screen was installed in 1924,
the three large ogival arches were omitted. The
church was built in 1902-1903 by William
Watson of Ascot; this perspective was drawn by
William Bucknall for the *Building News,* LXXXIII,
1902, p. 523, and was exhibited at the Royal
Academy in 1903.

Design for the completed church of St. Cyprian in St. Marylebone Middlesex. W. Bucknall & J. N. Comper Arch. & Old Jewry E. C.

not far from the contemporary work of his master Bodley, and he, too, put his creative energy into church decorative work, stained glass and textiles. By 1906, however, Comper had started to formulate his 'Unity by Inclusion' principle in St Mary's, Wellingborough, 1906-1930, where English Perpendicular is enriched by features and details from the Italian Renaissance and English Gothick, all combined with much gleaming decoration. Comper's designs for stained glass and working drawings for church decoration (a large number of which are at the RIBA) often give the impression of being drawn by a mediaeval artist or craftsman. It is interesting, by way of comparison, that Walter Tapper recalled that Bodley's drawings in his only sketchbook reminded him of 'William de Honnecourt's outline and were curiously out of drawing.'[12]

Another strong individualist in the Bodley office was Charles Robert Ashbee (1863-1942), one of the best known architects and craftsmen of the Arts and Crafts Movement. The knowledge of handicraft gained from Bodley, to whom he was articled in 1886, had a great effect on his later work. There are many sides to Ashbee's career. He founded the Guild and School of Handicraft in 1888 (first in the East End of London and then, in 1902, in Chipping Campden, Gloucestershire); he was a member of the Art Workers' Guild, restorer for SPAB, writer, designer of jewellery, metalwork and furniture, printer and bookbinder, the founder of the Essex House Press in 1898 and, finally, architect. Even his architectural work can be divided into three kinds: his restoration of churches and old buildings (the latter mainly in Chipping Campden); designs for new cottages; and designs for more original urban buildings in Chelsea. Drawings for these Chelsea buildings are to be found at the RIBA and at Chelsea Public Library.

In his own day Ashbee was not as noted for his architectural work as he is today. Lutyens, in a celebrated quotation, referred to Chipping Campden in 1906 as 'the headquarters of that most-to-me distasteful Ashbee, now artist — and furniture freakist'.[13] Nor did Muthesius put his architecture first: 'C.R. Ashbee, universally celebrated as an artist in metal, has built a number of houses in Chelsea, London, that have a certain distinctive quality though they are not always free of affectation. Ashbee is mainly occupied in directing his well-known Guild and School of Handicraft, with which he has now moved from London to the country. The pieces he makes there include domestic appointments such as furniture. His real strength, however, lies in the realm of metal utensils, for which he is justly celebrated.'[14] Ashbee's contemporaries possibly saw his Chelsea houses — of which only two survive today — as outré, arty versions of the Old London picturesque style, and not as they have been assessed in the last twenty years, as startlingly free examples of English Art Nouveau (Figs. 100, 102, 103 and colour plate XVI).

Charles Holden (1875-1960) was in the Ashbee office in 1897-1898, and in his *Memoirs*, Ashbee generously credited him with the design for Danvers Tower (Fig. 100). That Holden had been allowed to design at all shows how unusual the Ashbee office must have been, and a far cry from the relationship of master and pupil in the Bodley office, where Bodley would often give a pupil the dimensions of a design to work up which he had already designed in his head before putting pencil to paper.

Notes

1. Nikolaus Pevsner, *Staffordshire,* 1974, p. 148.
2. Edward Warren 'Architectural Draughts-manship', in the *RIBA Journal,* XXIX, 1922, p. 203.
3. Edward Warren 'The Life and Work of George Frederick Bodley', *RIBA Journal,* 1910, p. 334.
4. Walter Tapper in Edward Warren, *op. cit.,* p. 339.
5. Edward Warren, *op. cit.,* p. 334.
6. H.S. Goodhart-Rendel's Roll Call.
7. Nicholas Taylor 'Sir Albert Richardson: A Classic Case of Edwardianism' in Alastair Service *Edwardian Architecture and its Origins,* 1975, p. 448.
8. *Charles Canning Winmill* by his daughter, 1946, p. 22.
9. *Ibid.,* p. 54.
10. Peter Savage, *Lorimer and the Edinburgh Craft Designers,* 1980, p. 7.
11. *Ibid.,* pp. 67-68.
12. Walter Tapper in Edward Warren, *op. cit.,* p. 339.
13. Lutyens letters, 6 May, 1906 (LuE/8/2/1-12) RIBA MSS Collection.
14. Hermann Muthesius, *The English House,* p.119.

100 Charles Robert Ashbee (1863-1942). Design for 'Danvers Tower', on the corner of Cheyne Walk and Danvers Street, Chelsea, London, 1897. Pen and wash on tracing paper (520 x 735).

This is one of two alternative and 'advanced' designs at the RIBA for a scheme for a block of studios and flats for seven artists — John Tweed, Edwin Abbey, Ernest Oppler, John Singer Sargent, Augustus John and two others. Both schemes are dominated on the Cheyne Walk elevation by a striking white tower: note also the very 'Chelsea', artfully placed round windows, the use of white roughcast and vertical strips of windows. The design was turned down by the LCC, and is noted by Ashbee in his *Memoirs*: 'This was to stand at the corner of Danvers St where Crosby Hall now is, the drawings and much of the invention were by Charles Holden then working in my office.' (*The Ashbee Memoirs*, I, p. 111. Typescript in the Library at the Victoria and Albert Museum).

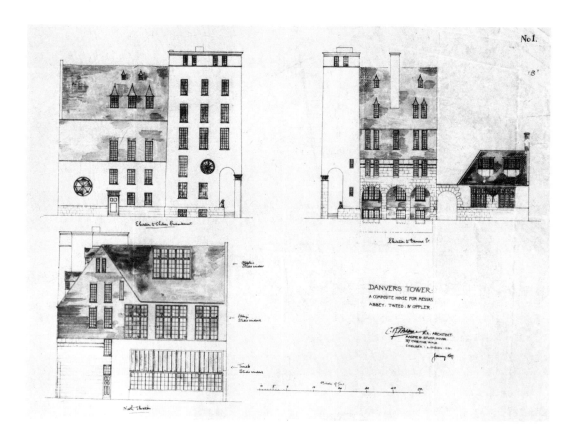

101 Charles H. Holden (1875-1960) working for H. Percy Adams (1866-1930). Preliminary design for the Belgrave Hospital for Children, Clapham Road, Kennington, London, *c*.1900. Pen and coloured washes (465 x 750).

Holden designed this hospital in a free neo-Tudor style while working as chief assistant in the office of H. Percy Adams. The design, although attributed formally to Adams, has many of Holden's characteristic motifs. The unexecuted frieze of figures above the entrance had appeared previously in his Soane Medallion design for a Provincial Market Hall of 1896 and the brick strips and buttresses, many of them set back on the upper levels, reappear in stone in his later classical designs, for example in the British Medical Association building on the Strand, 1907. The Arts and Crafts lettering, which replaced the frieze of figures, reads 'The Belgrave Hospital for Children / Supported by Voluntary Contributions.'

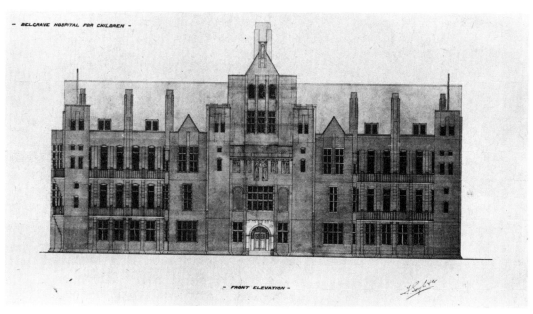

102 Charles Robert Ashbee, Design for Nos. 72-75 Cheyne Walk, Chelsea, London, 1897. Pen and wash with pencil on vellum (405 x 510).

In this design Ashbee wanted to create a picturesque river front that might give the impression of piecemeal development over a period of years. All the houses are different and their facades contain many of the motifs current in Chelsea since the establishment of 'Queen Anne' in the 1870s: artful round windows, canted bays, elongated oriel windows, all spread randomly to suggest a multitude of functions — double-height rooms, staircases, attic bedrooms or penthouse studios. Nos. 72-73 were built according to this design for the sculptor John Rollins and the Glasgow painter E.A. Walton respectively; No. 74, which was designed for Ashbee and his wife when they got married, was altered, when built, on the ground floor and No. 75, for a Mrs W. Hunt, was built by Ashbee to a quite different design in 1902. All four houses were destroyed by a parachute mine on the 17 April 1941.

103 Charles Robert Ashbee. Design for the men's hostel, The London Fraternity House, Shrewsbury Court, Nos. 40-45 Cheyne Walk, Chelsea, London, for the University of London, etched by Stanley Mercer, 1912. Etching (410 x 260).

Ashbee's 'London Fraternity House' would have occupied a narrow site next door to No. 39 Cheyne Walk. One would have entered through the archway in the perspective and would have passed through to the Married Hostel and Women's Hostel — both blocks being in Ashbee's version of the English Renaissance. Ashbee wanted 'to establish a community life as part of the University, and to link this up with the historic life of Chelsea, on the actual site of Sir Thomas More's garden, incorporating what was left of Shrewsbury House, the ancient Palace of Bess of Hardwick, one of the greatest of the Elizabethan builders.' (Ashbee, *Where the Great City Stands*, 1917, p. 84). The men's hostel, with its high tower, machicolations and windows set in brick between the vertical strips of stone, is one of the most forward-looking designs of the Movement. The scheme was never carried out.

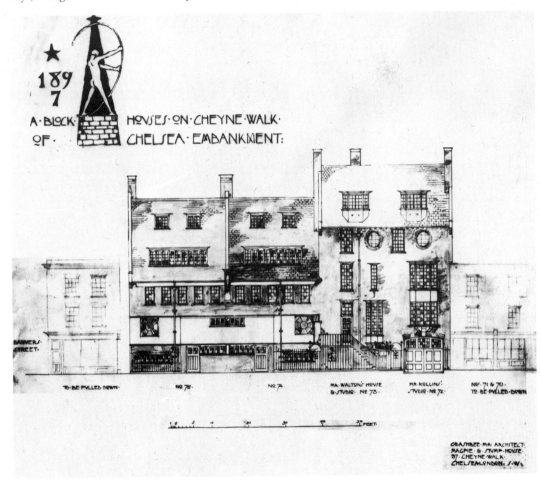

121

A Northern Group

Not all the leading Arts and Crafts architects had their practices in London. M.H. Baillie Scott, one of the most influential architects of the Movement, practised in the Isle of Man, and in the North of England until 1901. Walter H. Brierley worked in York, W.H. Bidlake in Birmingham, Herbert Luck North in North Wales, G.J. Skipper in Norwich and Francis W. Bedford and S.D. Kitson in Leeds; and one cannot begin to do justice to the Scottish movement in Glasgow in the 1890s which was headed by C.R. Mackintosh and George Walton.

Edgar Wood (1860-1935) was the leading Arts and Crafts architect in the North of England. He was born in Middleton near Manchester and articled to James Murgatroyd of the large Manchester firm, Mills and Murgatroyd. He set up in independent practice in 1885. Wood hated the time he had spent as a hack pupil in a large commercial architectural office and in his own practice adopted the role of the artist-architect. He had a small office, with one or two pupils and an office boy. G.A.E. Schwabe who went as pupil in 1893, and later remained with him until 1910, remembered that his first task on entering the office was to draw a bowl of roses.[1]

Throughout the whole of his career Wood's work was widely published in the the architectural journals, and particularly in the German press: a comprehensive record is to be found in *Moderne Bauformen,* Vol 6, No 2, 1908. Muthesius saw 'a pervasive poetical overtone in his designs which set him apart from the great majority of the London Arts and Crafts people, the dominant note of whose work is plainness', and thought that he formed a 'bridge to the poetical and imaginative north of the British Isles, to Scotland.'[2] Nikolaus Pevsner, possibly influenced by Muthesius's view, is unremitting in his praise. He calls the First Church of Christ Scientist (Figs. 105, 106) 'one of the most original buildings of that time in England or indeed anywhere . . . It is a pioneer work, internationally speaking, of an Expressionism halfway between Gaudi and Germany about 1920, and it stands entirely on its own in England.'[3] At the same time Wood followed Morris's teachings possibly more closely than many of his London contemporaries who were open to a wider range of influences. His use of vernacular building forms for the First Church of Christ Scientist makes it one of the few buildings of the Movement to realize Morris's dictum that it would be from necessary and unpretentious buildings that the new architecture would spring.

Wood was a founder member of the Northern Art Workers' Guild, inaugurated by Walter Crane in 1896, and its master in 1897. He worked as a craftsman and designed furniture, jewellery and metalwork. Up till about 1903-1904 his buildings followed the vernacular traditions of the Pennine region. The exterior of Banney Royd, near Huddersfield (1900-1901), in its rough-hewn stone, exactly matches the character of the ordinary houses of the hilly area. Wood's interiors were very similar to those by Baillie Scott. The Birkby Lodge interior (Fig. 104), for example, had much in common with the rooms Baillie Scott designed at the Grand Palace at Darmstadt, Hesse (1897-1898). Both have an 'architectural' system of decoration, with inglenooks, fitted furniture and painted friezes that found such favour in Germany. In 1903-1904 Wood was joined in an informal partnership by James Henry Sellers (1861-1954) and through him began to experiment with axial planning, classical detail and reinforced concrete. His later buildings, for example Upmeads, Stafford (1908), are symmetrical and have flat, concrete roofs.

George Walton (1867-1933) is the only architect in the RIBA Drawings Collection to

104 Edgar Wood (1860-1935). Design for the Dining Room, Birkby Lodge (now Hopkinson's Ltd.), Birkby Hall Road, Huddersfield, Yorkshire, for Mr Norton, 1901. Pencil and watercolour (280 x 445).

Although this design is, like many Arts and Crafts interiors, unified by the use of 'architectural' furnishings – dados, painted decoration, fixed sculpted panels above the fireplace, fixed seats and inglenooks – it is also particularly old-fashioned. It is directly reminiscent of an aesthetic Pre-Raphaelite interior of the 1860s, for example the Dining Room of Philip Webb's No. 1 Palace Green, Kensington (1868-1869), which has a similar dado and frieze illustrating Morris's *The Earthly Paradise* designed by Burne-Jones and painted by Walter Crane. Wood had always admired William Morris and the scene in the frieze (which depicts the Arthurian legend of the Holy Grail), showing the knights seated at a banquet, when they see 'A beam of light seven times more clear than day: and down the long beam stole the Holy Grail', is directly based on a Morris tapestry of the same subject at Stanmore Hall. Even the chequered inlay on the sideboard and dado echo the earlier work of Godwin and George Jack. Wood did, however, have his own strong views on the use of colour decoration for interiors (*see* Jill Lever *Architects' Designs for Furniture,* 1982, p. 107). He preferred fixed mural paintings to portable 'carry about' art, which could be hung in one place as well as another, and had used painted friezes before in his earlier houses of the 1890s, Briarcourt, Huddersfield, and Redcroft, Middleton. His close friend Frederick W. Jackson (1859-1918) painted the frieze which has now been removed and is in the care of the John Rylands University Library, Manchester.

represent the work of Muthesius's beloved Glasgow School. Muthesius felt that only the Glasgow architects, along with Baillie Scott, conceived of the house as an organic whole to be designed consistently inside and out. He saw that these ideas had emerged with Baillie Scott, in the work of C.R. Mackintosh and Walton in Glasgow, and on the Continent — but that 'London remained stationary at the point to which Morris had taken it.'[4] It is quite true that English architects were emphatic in criticising as the 'Spook School' the Glasgow work which was exhibited at the Arts and Crafts Exhibition Society in 1896; it is also true that on the Continent, in Darmstadt and Vienna, architects particularly admired the work of Baillie Scott, Mackintosh and Walton — although Voysey was equally influential.

Walton, like Peter Behrens, was not trained as an architect. Born is Glasgow, he was the son of a painter and younger brother of the artist Edward A. Walton, an admirer of Whistler. He left school at fourteen and worked as a bank clerk, at the same time attending evening classes, probably at the Glasgow School of Art. In 1888 he gave up banking and opened an interior decoration and design firm: it was very successful and Walton did many decorating jobs in Glasgow between 1889 and 1896. In 1895 Miss Cranston employed him with J. and W. Guthrie and others to decorate her newly aquired tea rooms at 91 Buchanan Street, and in 1896 was in charge of the project when Mackintosh received his first commission for mural decoration there. In 1898 Walton moved to London, where his principal client, George Davison, head of Kodak's European sales organisation, employed him to redecorate the Kodak offices at No. 4 Clerkenwell Street, London, and between then and 1902 to remodel the facades and interiors of a series of Kodak shops. He was admired on the Continent during this period: *Decorative Kunst* featured his interiors from 1900 and he was promoted by Muthesius.

In 1901 he turned his hand for the first time to a complete building, designing and building The Leys, Elstree (Fig. 107), for the portrait photographer J.B.B. Wellington. It is his best

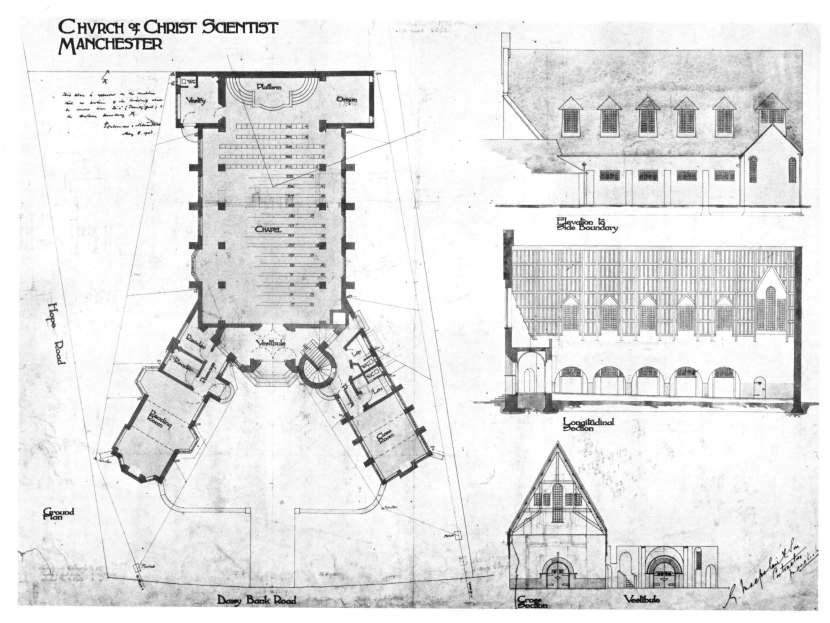

CHVRCH of CHRIST SCIENTIST MANCHESTER

105 Edgar Wood. Contract design for the First Church of Christ Scientist, Daisy Bank Road, Victoria Park, Manchester, 1903. Ground plan, side elevation and sections. Black and blue pen with coloured washes (610 x 830).

The plan takes the form of a symmetrical inverted Y, with the chapel in the centre and reading rooms and cloakrooms in the two wings. It is a variation of the 'butterfly' plan made popular by Prior's The Barn at Exmouth (1897) and much used by architects at this period in their house designs but never for ecclesiastical or urban buildings. The contract is dated 8 May 1903, although the church was not finished until 1908. The contractors were G. Macfarlane & Son from Manchester.

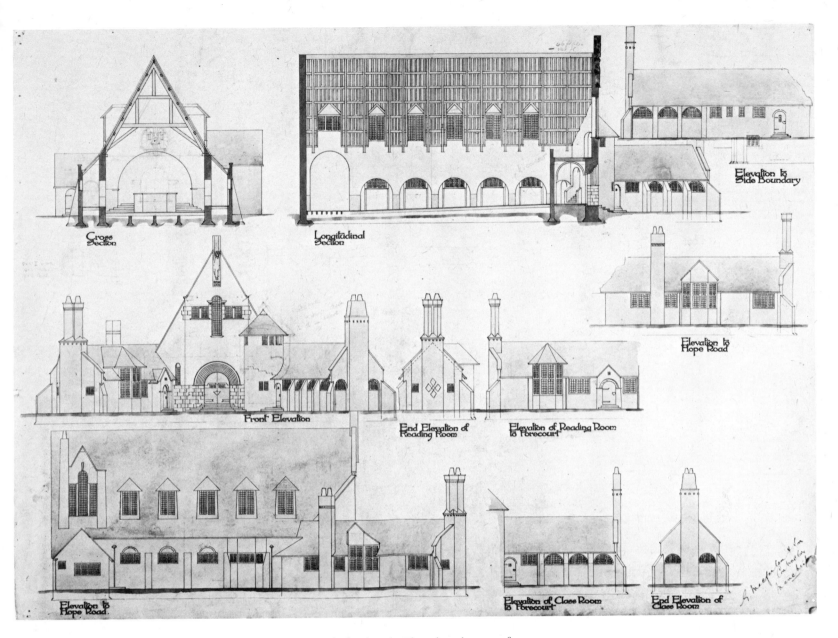

Cross Section

Longitudinal Section

Elevation to Side Boundary

Front Elevation

End Elevation of Reading Room

Elevation of Reading Room to Forecourt

Elevation to Hope Road

Elevation to Hope Road

Elevation of Class Room to Forecourt

End Elevation of Class Room

106 Edgar Wood. Contract design for the First Church of Christ Scientist, Daisy Bank Road, Victoria Park, Manchester, 1903. Elevations and sections. Pen and coloured washes (560 x 780).

The secular nature of the Christian Science church has allowed Edgar Wood to apply the vernacular forms of domestic building to an ecclesiastical structure. Only the exaggeratedly steep gable (a house gable), with its intersecting window forming a crucifix, echoes the usual West end of a church. The other elements, for example the chimneys that terminate the wings and the canted bay of the reading room, are all drawn from vernacular building. The sole purpose of the conically-capped tower flanking the entrance is to carry a staircase to the organ loft, but it adds interest and wilfulness to the elevation. This design does not show a high brick chimney which was later added behind the tower. The church was built of brick with stone dressings and roughcast on the gable.

107 George Walton (1867-1933). Design for The Leys, Barnet Lane, Elstree, Hertfordshire, for J.B.B. Wellington, 1901. Watercolour (750 x 560).

The Leys was Walton's first job as an architect; he had remodelled the facades of several Kodak shops in the late 1890s but had never tackled a complete building. The house is all the more remarkable for that, although at the time Walton was still acting as Managing Director of his Glasgow firm, George Walton and Co., and may have had the practical help of his builder partners. The Company made all the chimney-pieces and metalwork for the house. The client, J.B.B. Wellington, was a distinguished photographer and the first manager of the Kodak works at Harrow. This perspective, in Walton's free and painterly style, shows the garden side of the house. Although it had a hipped roof and was built of tile, brick and roughcast, the symmetry of the elevation and its division into three clearly defined horizontal bands make it one of the most progressive buildings of its date. The central curved entrance porch may derive from a similar two storey bow window at Voysey's Broadleys. The window on the far right of the first floor is blind — presumably an architectural conceit in the manner of Lutyens. Wellington was a keen billiard player, so the interior of the house is dominated by the centrally placed and triple-height billiard hall. The staircase rose from this hall and was separated from it by a screen of oak uprights, reminiscent both of Voysey and of Mackintosh's work at the Glasgow School of Art. The light fittings, fireplaces and metalwork at The Leys have the quality of Walton's best decorative work. The house was extended by Walton in 1923-1924 and has now been remodelled by the London Borough of Barnet as a hostel for the mentally handicapped. All the 'architectural' features survive but the fittings no longer exist.

108 Richard Barry Parker (1867-1947) and Sir Raymond Unwin (1863-1941). Design for a house on Windermere, Cumberland, for Edward Holt, *c.*1897-1898. Pen on card (365 x 445).

This unexecuted design for a luxurious house on Windermere, showing very clearly its American Shingle Style antecedents, provoked a caustic letter from M.H. Baillie Scott to the *Builder's Journal* in 1901. Parker and Unwin had made the design for Edward Holt, but he had been dissatisfied with it and had instead engaged Baillie Scott, whose design for 'Blackwells' was completed in 1901. Then on the 18 September, 1901, the *Daily Mail* published a review of Parker and Unwin's new book *The Art of Building a Home* (1901). The review illustrated three designs by Parker and Unwin each with price tags affixed to their roofs, and this perspective appeared with the caption 'A £10,000 Artistic House, built upon the same general plan as a middle class residence, but embellished in an extremely sumptuous manner inside and out.' The theme of the review was that for the sum of £500 a man of moderate income could obtain as pleasant a house as the huge residence costing £10,000. Baillie Scott strongly objected to this form of advertising under the general title 'How to Build your House. Concerning the Coming Revolution in Domestic Architecture', and on the 25 September 1901, wrote a sharp letter to the *Builder's Journal*: 'Sir, Have you observed the coming revolution in domestic architecture as set forth in the *Daily Mail*? Have you noticed the new construction in our £10,000 article where arches appear without abutments and stone gables rest on glass? One assumes a chapter 'On the Constructional Use of Window Panes' . . . Here is a very superior article indeed at £10,000 in which we have introduced the 'new construction'. No, it is not imported from America; it is of home manufacture, I assure you, Madame, all the work of our Mr De Parcy Sharper. But excuse me, did you not tell me just now that Mr De Sharper was an architect? Quite so, Madame. But I thought architects weren't supposed to advertise? Ah, Madame, that was before the revolution in domestic architecture. We have changed all that now! Yours truly, M.H. Baillie Scott.' One wonders if Baillie Scott knew that the £10,000 house illustrated was Parker and Unwin's rejected design for Edward Holt and which he had supplanted; Mervyn Miller, the Parker and Unwin specialist, feels he must have done.

work, and in its general massing and symmetry must be the prime source for Peter Behrens's Cuno House at Eppenhausen (1910). After 1901 Walton did little architectural work that had the quality of The Leys, although Raymond McGrath preferred the White House, Shiplake (1908), for its open plan and floor to ceiling glass doors. After 1914 he had few commissions; he was assistant architect to the Central Control Board for liquor traffic from 1916-1921, and made textile designs for Morton Sundour Fabrics from 1927-1930. The RIBA has a large collection of his designs for stained glass, war memorials, glass and furniture, decorative work and architecture; the drawings are sketched or painted in a free and colourful and unarchitectural hand.

Barry Parker (1867-1947) and Raymond Unwin (1863-1941) were also Northerners, close friends of Edgar Wood and members of the Northern Art Workers' Guild. They were second cousins, and both were born in the North of England, Parker at Chesterfield, Derbyshire, and Unwin at Rotherham, Yorkshire. Parker went to the South Kensington School of Art in London in 1886 (where he would have met Lutyens and Detmar Blow), studied interior design with T.C. Simonds of Derby from 1887-1889 and later was articled to the Manchester architect Faulkner Armitage from 1889-1893. Unwin grew up in Oxford but returned to the North to become an engineer and later architect for Stavely Iron and Coal Company near Chesterfield. In 1896 they began their practice together in Buxton. It consisted mainly of smaller houses which were obviously too modest for Muthesius's taste, who did not include them in his survey. Parker and Unwin were Socialists. Inspired by the ideals of Ruskin and Morris and the Utopian community ideas of Edward Carpenter, they remained faithful to a simple vernacular style and made their aim to improve the houses of the working classes. In their writings — particularly in *The Art of Building a Home* (1901) — they sought to popularise the Arts and Crafts Movement, and as a result thousands of moderate 'artistic' homes were built on their pattern in the early years of this century (Figs. 108, 109).

In 1902 they were asked by Joseph and Seebohm Rowntree to design a model village at New Earswick near York, and this led in the following year, to an invitation to submit a plan to

109 Richard Barry Parker and Sir Raymond Unwin. Design for the interior of the Hall for a house on Windermere for Edward Holt, *c.*1897-1898. Pen on card (320 x 420).

Parker and Unwin, together with Baillie Scott, pioneered the use of open plan living rooms in England. In this rather overstretched design the Hall has become the main living area of the house, and its spaces have been run together in the manner of the American 'Shingle Style' houses which were increasingly published in the English journals in the late 1880s. They said that 'if your big room is to be comfortable it *must* have recesses. There is a great charm in a room broken up in plan, where that slight feeling of mystery is given to it which arises when you cannot see the whole room from any one point in which you are likely to sit: when there is always something *round the corner.*' (*The Art of Building a Home,* 1901). The drawing also shows Parker's odd style of draughtsmanship which is characterised by a method of cross-hatching which often disturbs the planes of the perspective but adds to a feeling of rough-hewn simplicity.

the First Garden City Company for the development of their site at Letchworth. Early in 1904 their plan was adopted and the practice opened a second office at Baldock. In 1905 they were asked by Henrietta Barnett to plan the new Garden Suburb at Hampstead, and in 1906 Unwin moved from Letchworth to Hampstead where he lived for the remainder of his life. Parker designed and built his own office in Letchworth in 1906-1907 in the form of a thatched Mediaeval Hall house.[5] The Hall became the drawing office and the Solar the private office, with a discreet window through which to keep an eye on the assistants. It is one of the few tailor-made architectural offices of the Movement. Their assistants were given considerable freedom in design within the office, and then, when Letchworth and Hampstead were underway, were given commissions to set them up in independent practice — many of them for houses in the garden cities. From the Buxton and Letchworth offices came Courteney M. Crickmer, Cecil Hignett, S. Pointon Taylor, Robert Bennett and Wilson Bidwell, and from the Hampstead office at Wyldes Farm came Herbert Welch and F.J. Lander, Michael Bunney, C.C. Makins, T.M. Wilson, A.J. Penty and Charles Wade. The partnership continued on this basis with offices in Hampstead and Letchworth until 1914 when it was dissolved upon Unwin's appointment as Chief Inspector of Town Planning for the Local Government Board.

Notes

1. John Archer, 'Edgar Wood: a notable Manchester Architect', *Transactions of the Lancashire & Cheshire Antiquarian Society,* LXXIII-LXXIV, 1963-1964, pp. 153-187. J. Archer and S. Evans *Partnership in Style: Edgar Wood & J. Henry Sellers,* catalogue of an exhibition, Manchester City Art Gallery, 1975.
2. Hermann Muthesius, *The English House,* p. 47.
3. Nikolaus Pevsner *South Lancashire,* 1969, p. 48.
4. Hermann Muthesius, *op. cit.,* p. 51.
5. 296 Norton Way South, Letchworth, now containing the Garden City Museum (information from typescript notes by Mervyn Miller on an exhibition of Parker & Unwin at Letchworth).

110 Richard Barry Parker and Sir Raymond Unwin. Design for Chetwynd, Northwood, Clayton, Staffordshire for C.F. Goodfellow, 1899. Perspective of the inglenook of the living room, looking towards the small garden court. Pencil and watercolour on brown board (295 x 630).

This is the first house illustrated in *The Art of Building a Home* and is Parker and Unwin's first mature work. The clients had specified that the house should be adaptable for 'open-air living' and in consequence the plan is arranged around a small central courtyard into which all the doors opened. The living room formed the centre of the family's activities and meals were taken there in the bay window. The ingle had 'several small windows to afford peeps out towards the court and the view, and to give light, conveniently placed for anyone reading; also having cupboards for display of the client's collection of Oriental pottery which is being utilised, somewhat by way of decoration, where the changing lights falling on its bright colourings will give some additional variety to its beauty.' (*The Art of Building a Home*). The floors and fireback were constructed of blue-grey testellated tiles, the fireplace hood and fitted coal box were of copper and the wood of the over-mantel cabinets and settles stained dark brown (information from Mervyn Miller).

111 Richard Barry Parker and Sir Raymond Unwin. Design for No. 34 Sollershott West, Letchworth, Hertfordshire, 1908. Pen and watercolour (195 x 260).

The houses along Sollershott West were the more expensive ones in the garden city, well set back in spacious gardens. The design has the 'sun-trap' butterfly plan beloved of Arts and Crafts architects, and a formal, symmetrical garden with a circular rose-covered pergola in the centre.

112 Temple Lushington Moore (1856-1920). Design for the Church of All Saints, Park Road, Peterborough, Northamptonshire, 1886-1894, completed in 1903. Pencil and sepia wash (695 x 465).

The interior of this early Moore church shows both the influence of his master George Gilbert Scott Junior and his own highly personal style. Like Scott's St Agnes, Kennington, it copies the spirit not the letter of the 14th century, and has the same vaulted wooden roof, square-topped nave windows and no capitals to the arcades. It is, however, as Pevsner has stated 'quite original' in its lofty arcade, simplified piers and unusual plan — for the North aisle is uncommonly wide and there is no South aisle. H.C. Corlette particularly remembered it for its interesting brick interior, which he compared to Albi, and thought it was a building well worth seeing (*RIBA Journal*, XXXV, 1928, p. 491).

The Temple Moore Office and other church architects

Temple Lushington Moore (1856-1920) was the pupil of George Gilbert Scott Junior and gradually took over his practice after his master became insane in 1883. He too worked in a late Gothic style but his work has a greater strength and simplicity than Scott's or Bodley's. Goodhart-Rendel said that 'Moore spoke Gothic with a strong Yorkshire accent':[1] he adapted the austerity of the Yorkshire Cistercian abbeys of Byland and Roche to many churches all over England. It was a large practice; he designed thirty-eight new churches, added to twenty-seven and restored forty-seven, as well as designing several secular buildings.

Moore was not a member of the Art Workers' Guild and his work does not have any of the more obvious Arts and Crafts decorative features. Nonetheless he finds a place in this book for his very lack of stylism, for his austerity and, above all, for his masterly handling of materials. Goodhart-Rendel noted that 'the stonework of the walls at St Wilfred's, Harrogate [his finest church, 1905-1914] has the most beautiful texture imaginable, and such tooled ashlar as this, with its irregular courses and bold joints, is constantly to be found in buildings of his design.'[2] He also used brick, occasionally rubble and designed church furniture and fittings.

Giles Gilbert Scott (1880-1960), the son of George Gilbert Scott Junior, was articled to Moore in 1898 with his brother Adrian. In 1901 he entered the preliminary competition for Liverpool Cathedral and was still a pupil when, to his great surprise, he found himself one of the five selected to submit designs. In 1903 he was the winner. Scott's early churches, many of them much overshadowed by Liverpool, owe much to Moore's simplified Gothic in their massing and plain walls, although in their texture and flamboyant Gothic details are closer to contemporary Arts and Crafts work (Fig. 113).

Moore did not have an office in the conventional sense. He himself always worked at home in Well Walk, Hampstead, but his pupils worked under the supervision of his office manager P.B.F. Freeman in an office in Staple Inn which was shared with five other architects all carrying on their own practices. He only visited Staple Inn periodically; he was as Scott remembered him extraordinarily quiet and retiring and was of a rather nervous disposition. He lived almost a hermit's life in Hampstead and did not enter into the politics of architects. 'He seemed to know and care little of what was going on in the architectural world generally, being entirely wrapped up in his work.'[3] Leslie Thomas Moore, who was in partnership with Moore from 1919-1920 and whose son-in-law and successor he became, recalled that his 'lefthandedness in drawing was quite remarkable; to see him draw with his two hands, holding the rubber in his mouth, was most interesting. He always worked until 11 o'clock at night, dictating letters which Mrs Moore wrote, and specifications, too. He had very few architectural books. I do not remember seeing him read any book, except one, and that was Viollet-le-Duc's *Dictionary of Architecture*.'[4]

In 1895 William Douglas Caröe (1857-1938) was appointed architect to the Ecclesiastical and Charity Commission and, like Moore, a vast amount of church work passed through his hands. He was architect to several cathedrals, including Canterbury and Durham, restored countless ecclesiastical buildings as well as being the designer of many new churches, the most

113 Giles Gilbert Scott (1880-1960). Design for
the Roman Catholic Church of Our Lady Star of
the Sea and St Maughold and presbytery,
Ramsey, Isle of Man, 1909. Watercolour
(460 x 560).

Standing on an exposed site facing the sea, this
church with its adjoining presbytery shows
Scott's liking for simple masses and plain walls. It
has much in common with his other early
churches at Bournemouth and Sheringham, and
the tall belfry window is of similar form to the
transept windows at Liverpool Cathedral. The
external walls are hollow, the outer thickness
being of rubble (obtained from old buildings
demolished on the site) and the interior of
smooth local bricks, limewashed. The heavily
textured effect of the rubble walls is not
adequately conveyed in this perspective. The
interior is quite plain — save for the Stations of
the Cross and a gilded and coloured triptych.
The builders were Messrs Sherwin and Son of
Boston, Lincolnshire. St Maughold was Bishop of
the Isle of Man; he was a pirate in Ireland, told
by St Patrick to put to sea in a coracle without
oars as a penance for his misdeeds and landed
on the island.

114 William Douglas Caröe (1857-1938). Design
for the Church of St Stephen, Bobbers Mill
Road, Nottingham, 1896. Pen and coloured
washes (495 x 665).

An early Caröe design and one that is typical of
his free Arts and Crafts Gothic. The church has
very low aisles, a fanciful turret, broad windows,
inventive tracery and a West elevation with a
buttress right up the centre of the central window
— a motif taken from the west front of Henry
Wilson's St Peter's, Ealing (1892).

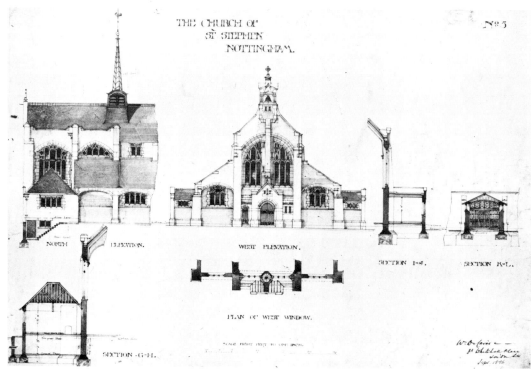

115 Sir Aston Webb (1849-1930). Design for the Church of St George, St George's Square, Worcester, drawn by T. Raffles Davison, 1893. Sepia pen (305 x 380).

Pevsner calls this church of 1893-1895 'a key work of his early and best period . . . nothing, except the window tracery, is really imitative.' Its design follows the Sedding-Wilson pattern of Holy Trinity, Sloane Street (based on King's College Chapel), that is basically a large Perpendicular window flanked by towers and again by low aisles, and surmounted by a towerlet. In this drawing, however, the towers have become massive buttresses rising to a flat roof, a motif which just predates Henry Wilson's influential design for the West front of St Andrew's Boscombe, Bournemouth of 1895. The drawing differs in details from the executed building.

Notes

1. H.S. Goodhart-Rendel, 'The Work of Temple Moore', in the *RIBA Journal*, XXXV, 1928, p. 473.
2. *op. cit.*, p. 484.
3. *op. cit.*, p. 487.
4. *op. cit.*, p. 490-491.
5. B.F.L. Clarke 'Edwardian Ecclesiastical Architecture' in Alastair Service *Edwardian Architecture and its origins*, 1975, p. 294.
6. J.D. Kornwolf *M.H. Baillie Scott and the Arts and Crafts Movement*, 1972, p. 402.

interesting of which are St David's, Exeter, and St George's, Leicester. Although he had been trained by J.L. Pearson and was a devoted admirer of his work, his own buildings showed more the influence of Sedding and Wilson and the Art Workers' Guild (of which he was a member in 1890), and were in his own highly personal version of a free Arts and Crafts Perpendicular (Fig. 114). According to Basil Clarke he enlivened this style 'with many improvisations such as buttresses which run up the mullions of windows, and arches of odd shapes, not unlike the peculiarities of E.B. Lamb fifty years earlier. Caröe's brickwork, if it has not Virginia Creeper growing on it, always looks as though it ought to have.'[5]

Aston Webb's design for St George's Church, Worcester (Fig. 115), also showed the influence of Sedding, and was an early version of a free Arts and Crafts Gothic that came to be peculiarly associated with Henry Wilson's Boscombe Church design, which it in fact precedes.

Webb (1849-1930) is not usually linked with the Arts and Crafts Movement. He practised in a variety of styles — 'Jacobean', 'Franco-Flemish', 'François Premier' — and ran a large office. His work was an anathema to the more avant-garde, and it was professional gossip at one time that he never had less than two million pounds worth of work on hand. Baillie Scott referred to his school as the 'Webb-ed foot' in architecture.[6] He is best known for the Admiralty Arch, Whitehall (1903-1910) and the refacing of Buckingham Palace in 1912.

116 Charles Edward Mallows (1864-1915). Design for a house on the River Severn at Upton, Worcestershire, for James Seaforth, 1888. Pen on board (465 x 340).

This particular drawing was exhibited at the Royal Academy in 1888 and illustrated in the *Building News* in that year. Goodhart-Rendel rather caustically noted that it 'must have introduced most of the readers of that journal for the first time to the young perspective artist who was afterwards to attain such phenomenal popularity, C.E. Mallows. I am afraid that I think that all that was respectable in the work of Rico and Pennell was absent in his, and that his wonderful adroitness would have been better employed in almost any direction than that in which he turned it. However, the dazzle technique dazzled English architects very completely, every senior draughtsman practising its tricks with the hope some day of becoming another Mallows!' (*RIBA Journal*, LVIII, 1951, p. 133). But Mallows's drawings are some of the most effective of the Movement in conveying a romantic impression of buildings already well established over the years in natural settings. It is hard to remember that this is a design for a new building and not a topographical drawing. The house has not been traced.

The Office of William Flockhart

William Flockhart (*c.* 1850-1913) is a somewhat enigmatic figure. He was a Scottish architect who practised in London, but of whom very little is known to date. He built several large houses in Scotland, and houses and business premises in London — notably No. 2 Palace Court, Bayswater (1891), which is in a mannered eclectic style. Goodhart-Rendel, however, remembered him as an 'extremely sensitive draughtsman, potentially the best of the lot. His architecture was inventive and original.'[1] His office, moreover, was probably the most 'artistic' of the period, for his leading pupils — Mallows, Adshead and Oliver Hill — not only inherited his skill in draughtsmanship but also his ability to conjure up appropriate styles for different jobs.

Stanley Davenport Adshead (1868-1947), who was in the office in the 1890s and who learnt there much of his skill as a perspective artist, has provided a vivid description of Flockhart: 'He was a man with a highly strung and very artistic temperament . . . and a skilled draughtsman and watercolour artist. I have learned more from him than from anyone. He thoroughly understood the uses of bodycolour, of ruling architectural drawings with a T-square and a brush. He could make beautiful drawings of interiors of furnished rooms and was adept at showing tapestries and plush . . . Few architects possessed his knowledge of Louis Quinze and Quatorze and other semi-decadent English styles. These gave him the opportunity for originality of composition, and did not tie him down to the severity of pure style.' Flockhart designed *everything* himself, and often rubbed out a pupil's drawing and made him do it again. This sometimes produced what nearly amounted to a strike in the back office; Flockhart made peace by 'buying off'— he wrote out cheques and said 'Let us be good friends.'[2]

Charles Edward Mallows (1864-1915) would have been one of Flockhart's first pupils in London in *c.* 1885. He had been in other offices and in 1886 set up on his own, first with F.W. Lacey and later with George Grocock with whom he established a practice in Bedford for some years. He could turn his hand to many styles — Art Nouveau (Fig. 117), Arts and Crafts vernacular (Figs. 116, 117 and colour plate XIX), Georgian or classical for public buildings, but is probably most associated with the full blown Elizabethan manner of his largest country house, Tirley Garth, Willington, Cheshire (1906). He is better known, however, for his skill as an architectural draughtsman and, with his pupil F.L. Griggs, could convey the random textures of houses and gardens far better than anyone else of his generation.

Frederick Landseer Griggs (1879-1938) was articled to Mallows in 1896 until he abandoned architecture for drawing in 1898. Even after that he kept up the association and continued to draw perspectives for Mallows for some years (Figs. 118, 119). In 1903 Griggs went to live and work in Chipping Campden where Ashbee had just established his Guild of Handicraft, and came to be associated with the Cotswold School. At first he lived in Dover's House in the main street and in *c.* 1927 designed a new house for himself, with the same name, a short distance away. He had it built by Cotswold masons using traditional methods. He used to boast that he only supplied them with a sketch design, and that there was not a straight line or a right-angle in the house. He worked with Gimson and contributed several woodcuts to *Ernest Gimson: His Life and Work*, 1924. As well as producing many drawings, woodcuts and etchings of buildings and landscape, Griggs founded the Campden Trust with Norman Jewson and others in 1929 and did much to preserve the town.

117 Charles Edward Mallows and George
Grocock. Design for an opera house in Bedford
for Carl St Amory, c.1895. Pen on board
(615 x 440).

Mallows made another design for the proposed
opera house, also in Art Nouveau style; dated
1895, it was exhibited at the Royal Academy in
1896. Carl St Amory (1851-1926), a Danish
musician and composer, was a Bedford resident
who since his arrival from Copenhagen in 1890,
had enlivened cultural life in Bedford. He
commissioned Mallows and Grocock to design
an opera house to be erected on the corner of
St Cuthbert's and Lurke Street. It was an unusual
design for Mallows and for England generally,
with its Art Nouveau decoration, and was never
executed.

118 Charles Edward Mallows and George
Grocock. Design for the garden shelter and lily
pond at Three Gables, No. 17 Biddenham Turn,
Biddenham, Bedfordshire, for H.J. Peacock,
drawn by Frederick Landseer B. Griggs
(1876-1938), 1901. Pen (360 x 290).

Simple pools, with the water brought up nearly
to the ground level, gave variety to enclosed
courts and were much used in gardens of this
period. Particularly important were the
reflections. The lily pond and shelter shown here
were intended to be placed between the tennis
lawn on one side and the kitchen garden on the
other, divided from both by formal yew hedges.

119 Charles Edward Mallows and George Grocock. Perspective of Three Gables, No. 17, Biddenham Turn, Biddenham, Bedfordshire, for H.J. Peacock, drawn by Frederick Landseer Griggs, 1909. Pencil (225 x 145).

'Three Gables' was included in Gertrude Jekyll and Lawrence Weaver's *Gardens for small country houses*, 1912, as a good example of a house that had a close connection between house and garden. The garden side gave the house its name, with three gables facing onto a terrace; this view is of the North West corner and shows Mr Peacock's study on the right and a tall, oriel, staircase window. The house was designed and built in 1900-1901 for Mallows's father-in-law. The textures of tile and brick and the 'enclosing comfort' of an English garden are well suggested by Griggs's soft pencil drawing.

Oliver Hill belongs to another generation. He was Flockhart's pupil from 1907-1910 and at the same time attended evening classes at the Architectural Association where he learnt to design in the Beaux-Arts manner. Hill is noted for his ability to design in a bewildering number of styles, and one wonders if he learnt this from Flockhart. He designed Lutyenesque houses such as Cour House, Argyllshire (1920-1921, Fig. 121), Georgian town houses like Wilbrahim House, Chelsea (1922) and houses such as Joldwynds, Holmbury St Mary, Surrey (1924) in the International style. He also had a reputation for extravagant interiors and was particularly noted for his luxurious bathrooms and boudoirs. Hill did, however, have a strong puritan streak that ran through his work and which he had inherited form the Arts and Crafts Movement. Both Lutyens and *Country Life* had meant a lot to him during his boyhood and at Lutyens's suggestion he worked in a builder's yard for eighteen months after leaving school. The First World War interrupted the early years of his practice, but during the the 1920s he built many houses which followed the patterns established by the Movement in the 1890s. Hills's clients, however, seemed richer and so he was able to use the most expensive materials, like oak, with the traditional building methods and craftsmanship that still existed during the inter-war period (Figs. 122, 123). After the Second World War he settled in Ernest Gimson's Daneway House, Sapperton (an ancient Cotswold manor which had been Gimson's workroom and showroom), which he skilfully restored. The house presented the romantic, twentieth century picture of the Arts and Crafts Movement with its bare boards, dried flowers and oak furniture, arranged with unlimited expense and expertise. It epitomised Oliver Hill's dual nature, for he was the kind of architect who drove a Chrysler at 50mph in the 1930s but made his own envelopes. It was a perfect Cotswold house, set in a beautiful garden; but tucked in a secluded arbour and approached by a narrow path was a small, bright blue swinmming pool.

Notes

1. 'Goodhart-Rendel's Roll-Call' in Alastair Service, *Edwardian Architecture and its origins*, 1975, p. 478.
2. 'Architects I have known': The architectural career of S.D. Adshead. Edited by Alan Powers in *Architectural History*, Volume 24, 1981, pp. 113-114.

120 Frederick Landseer Griggs (1879-1938). Topographical drawing of East Mascalls, Lindfield, Sussex, 1903. Pen (125 x 195). Inscribed on the mount: *East Mascalls before Restoration.*

Griggs was noted for his topographical drawings of which this is a good example. He had abandoned architecture for drawing in 1898 and in 1900 was approached with an offer to illustrate the Hertfordshire volume of the 'Highways and Byways' series of topographical guides, published by Macmillan. In all he illustrated thirteen volumes in the series. The drawing is also interesting as showing an Elizabethan house in an extraordinary state of disrepair compared with the standards of today. It was the type of building that Philip Webb and William Morris at SPAB fought to repair with sensitivity and save from wholesale restoration. The drawing was given to the RIBA in 1942 by Mrs Walter Millard, the wife of the architect who gave Griggs his first drawing lessons.

121 Oliver Hill (1887-1968). Design for the Cour, Kintyre, Argyllshire, 1921. Pencil, black and white chalk and gum arabic (400 x 530).

Oliver Hill fought in the First World War as an officer in the London Scottish Regiment, but soon found clients after the war. The Cour is a large mansion situated on the remote Argyll peninsular and was designed and built in the early 1920s. It is still basically a house that derives from the pre-war Arts and Crafts tradition but is more streamlined in its curving roofs and forms. The plan, and much more, derive from Lutyens. The front door is flanked by circular towers containing a gun room and staircase; the elevation is then terminated by projecting wings containing changing rooms and a servants' hall which are brought forward, in the manner of Lutyens's Tigbourne Court, to act as symmetrical lodges. On entering, the visitor immediately faces a blank wall (very Lutyens) and is forced to turn immediately to the right to find the Hall. Although its tall, unmoulded chimneys and regular rounded windows derive from no local precedent, its conically-capped towers echo the vernacular traditions of Scottish castles of the 15th and 16th centuries. It was also built of local blue-grey Whin stone quarried on the site, (in true Prior fashion) and roofed in slate. It remains one of the finest and least-known houses of the Inter-War period.

THE ENTRANCE FRONT
HOUSE IN ARGYLLSHIRE

122 Oliver Hill. Design for Fox Steep, Holly Cross, Wargrave, Berkshire, for Donald van den Bergh, 1924. Pencil (315 x 460).

Fox Steep was designed as 'a weekend retreat, within easy motor ride of town,' and is a skilful exercise — almost a *tour de force* — in building traditionally. It was a total rebuilding and enlargement of an existing 17th century inn. The outside walls were clad in waney elm weatherboarding, of silver grey hue, the chimneys were of Dutch bricks and there were oak window frames and leaded-light windows. The woodwork inside was of expensive oak — in the form of half-timbering, stairs with carved newel-posts, doors and two-foot wide floor planks, and the chimneypieces elaborate exercises in bricklaying. But there are also contrasts in keeping with the age: the interior decoration was by Albert Van der Velde — who introduced daffodil yellow walls, jade carpeting and black-leaded ceilings. A typical Hill bathroom consisted of a bath in the shape of a fountain which was lined with jade-coloured mosaic. Pevsner called the house 'a Hansel and Gretel fantasy'.

123 Oliver Hill. Design for Woodhouse Copse, Holmbury St Mary, Surrey, 1924. Pen and pencil on tracing paper (370 x 750).

In the 1920s Hill re-used the form of the thatched vernacular cottage for a number of his houses, combining moulded thatch with waney clapboard to good effect. Roderick Gradidge has pointed out that the highly plastic use of thatch was something that Hill and the Amsterdam School seemed to develop separately but in parallel in the 1920s. Vornick and Wormster's Villa 't Reigersnest at Oostvoorne near Rotterdam (1920) is remarkably similar to this design and to Hill's thatched house at Croyde, North Devon, (1925). All three designs were almost certainly influenced by Lutyens's and Voysey's cottages at Ashby St Ledgers and Madresfield Court, which were much published, and Hill would also have known Gimson's thatched Leicestershire cottages.

124 Arnold Dunbar Smith (1866-1933) and
Cecil Claude Brewer (1871-1918). Competition
design for the side elevation (facing Little Coram
Street), of the Passmore Edwards Settlement
(now Mary Ward House), Tavistock Place,
London, 1895. Pen and coloured washes
(770 x 565).

In June 1895 Dunbar Smith and the young Cecil
Brewer, who was then only twenty four, won the
limited competition for a charitable building
which was to be partly a university hostel and
partly an adult educational and recreational
centre. The competition had been a cosy, almost
family, affair for the Arts and Crafts circle.
Eleven architects were invited to submit designs:
Smith and Brewer, M.S. Hack, Gerald Horsley,
A.H. Mackmurdo, E.W. Mountford, E. Newton,
E.S. Prior, H. Ricardo, W. Stirling, F.W. Troup,
F. Waller and H. Wilson. (Hack, Mackmurdo and
Waller did not submit.) The assessor was
R. Norman Shaw.
  Smith and Brewer's design had a good plan
which cleverly combined the dual function of the
building and was picturesque in a modern way.
It was very like a Maclaren building with its
domed tower and sculptured front door, and —
the ultimate in praise from Shaw — 'it looks like
what it is'. But an enormous change occurred
between 1895 and its execution in 1898. Is the
building as we know it, with its strong horizontal
roof line, symmetrical towers with diagonally
ascending windows and asymmetrically placed
front door, in fact the work of Smith and Brewer
or was the design 'guided' by Shaw or Lethaby?
We know that Shaw wanted to reverse the
position of the door and main window on the
Tavistock Place elevation, and there was general
dissatisfaction expressed at the quality of all the
designs in the *British Architect* at the time. This
competition elevation faced onto Little Coram
Street, which is no longer in existence: the main
façade had regularly spaced Georgian windows, a
mansard roof and a large tripartite window. Even
the doorways on both elevations only hint at
what is to come (Fig. 125).

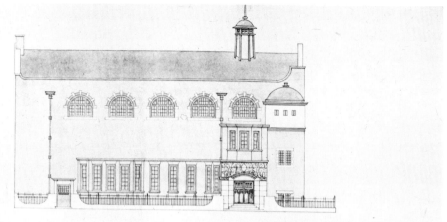

ELEVATION TOWARDS LITTLE CORAM STREET

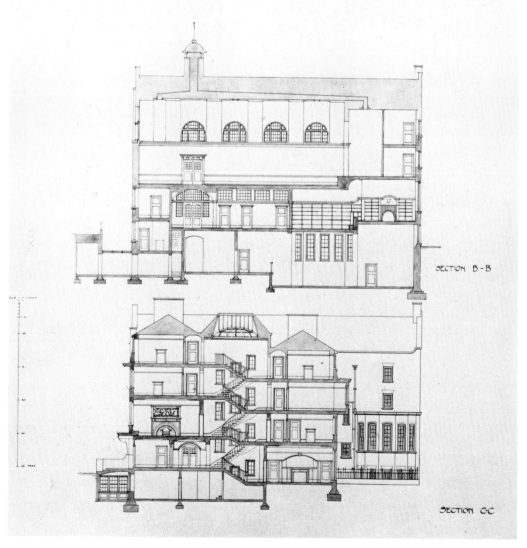

SECTION B-B

SECTION C-C

Successors

The successors of the leading architects of the Movement carried the style well on into the twentieth century. In about 1905 many, like Lutyens, turned increasingly to classicism, but the majority kept the vernacular as one of the styles in their repertoire, the others being Tudor and Georgian.

Arnold Dunbar Smith and Cecil Claude Brewer had both worked in a number of offices. Smith had been with Messrs Lilley, Mew, Frank Baggallay (who had trained with Sir Arthur Blomfield) and Walter Millard. Brewer had also been with Baggallay for three years and then had spent a year with Schultz. They were both residents at University Hall when they were invited to enter the limited competition for the new Passmore Edwards Settlement in 1895 (Figs. 124-125). As executed the building was one of the most original and influential of the Movement. Until 1909 when they won the competition for the National Museum of Wales in Cardiff, their work was mainly domestic alternating between a tasteful application of the vernacular (Fig. 126) and the full-blown Wrenaissance of Ditton Place, Balcombe, Sussex, 1904. Goodhart-Rendel found their work 'not very rational — but with enormous period charm'.

It is not easy to put Clough Williams-Ellis into any one category; he was too much of an individualist, and was certainly not a member of the Art Workers' Guild. He was not trained by the system of pupilage, and although he had spent a certain amount of time at the Architectural Association, was prouder of the fact that he had worked for a Sussex builder, as

125 Arnold Dunbar Smith and Cecil Claude Brewer. Design for the Principal Entrance and interior details, Passmore Edwards Settlement (now Mary Ward House), Tavistock Place, London, c.1897. Pen and coloured washes (550 x 780).

The Principal Entrance is the outstanding feature of the Mary Ward Settlement. The stone porch with its curving walls rising from the pavement is more original and 'organic' than anything in England of this date. It is topped by two stone eggs (one of which is visible in this drawing) which are the symbols of creation suggested by Lethaby's *Architecture, Mysticism and Myth*, 1891.

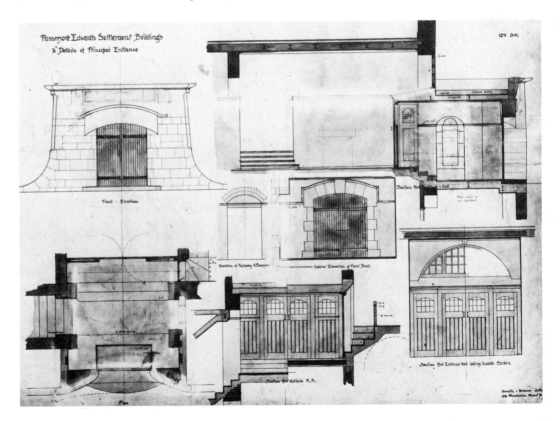

126 Arnold Dunbar Smith (1866-1933) and
Cecil Claude Brewer (1871-1918). Design for The
Sundial, Holmwood, Surrey, for F.W. Pethick
Lawrence, 1903. Pen and coloured wash
(510 x 680).

This cottage was built as a children's country
holiday cottage for F.W. Pethick Lawrence, who
lived nearby at 'La Mascot' (now called The
Dutch House), South Holmwood, which had
been designed by Lutyens in 1901 and also had a
Y shaped plan. It has a 'primitive simplicity' and
'tastefulness' which Muthesius recognized as the
principal qualities in their work.

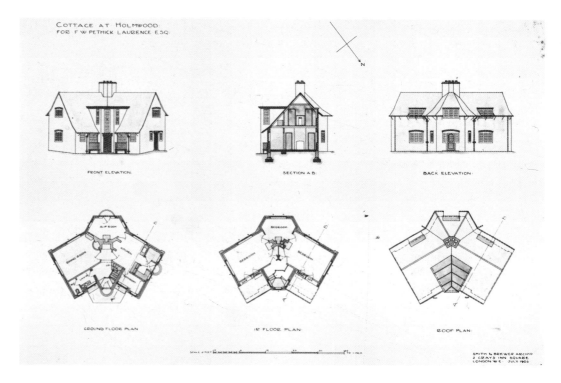

Lutyens had done. From as early as 1905 he was making designs for cheap cottages (Fig. 128),
possibly at the Architectural Association, and this interest in practical building materials and
old cottage structures, and the lessons to be learnt from them for contemporary needs, stayed
with him all his life. In 1908 he inherited the family property at Plas Brondanw in North Wales
and put his whole skill as an architect into rebuilding the house and estate. His love for
'abiding materials' — be they vernacular or classical as long as innately Welsh or English led
to his interest in preserving Snowdon and in the conservation of old buildings which is part of
the fantasy of Portmeirion.

Edward Brantwood Maufe served a five year pupilage with William A. Pite from 1899. In
the early years of the century his family had moved south to live in William Morris's former
home, the Red House, Bexley Heath, which Maufe acknowledged as an early architectural
influence. Kelling Hall (Fig. 129) was his first large commission and shows his early links with
the Movement in its butterfly plan, knapped flint walls and gabled roof. After the First World
War his work became influenced by Swedish architecture, which he much admired and his
buildings came to have a stylish modernity in direct contrast to the new functionalism.

By contrast A.J. Penty was one of several architects (Charles Spooner included) who in the
1920s advocated a return to the vernacular as a basis for design — a revival of the rational
building days of the 1890s. He had been articled to his father in York and together had
established a large practice, Penty and Penty, specializing in Arts and Crafts style houses. After
his father's death in 1902 he moved to the London area and worked for Parker and Unwin on
Hampstead Garden Suburb. He was a Fabian and wrote a number of socially-based articles
expounding his views in relation to architecture, notably, 'The restoration of the guild system'
in which he proposed a return to mediaeval guild practice in architecture, which would

127 Arnold Dunbar Smith and Cecil Claude Brewer. Design for a cottage to cost £150 for the Cheap Cottages Exhibition at Letchworth, 1905, built in permanent form with additions in Norton Road, Letchworth, Hertfordshire. Print, with coloured washes (330 x 490).

In 1905 John St Loe Strachey (1860-1927), proprietor and editor of *The Spectator*, organized the Cheap Cottages Exhibition at Letchworth in order to encourage progress in cottage building. For some years there had been a great shortage of living accommodation for agricultural workers. Few cottages were being built because it cost more to build a cottage than a labourer could afford to pay in rent. Strachey therefore felt it was essential to reduce the cost of a dwelling to £150 — which enabled it to be let at between 3s 6d and 4s per week, which was all the labourer could afford. To do this he wanted to change the Building By-laws, which prevented cottages being erected of other materials than brick or stone. The exhibition was set up to experiment with different methods of construction, and prizes were given to different categories. The £150 cottage was the most important class: it was to comprise a living room, scullery and three bedrooms. The winner was Percy Houfton; Smith and Brewer won second prize for this design in a sub-category for wooden cottages. Their cottage had walls of weatherboarding and a pantile roof. A small bay window, 'such as may be seen in old cottages of the neighbourhood' was the only picturesque feature; the width of the building was kept the same throughout to simplify its construction. Its design was based on a cottage they had built in 1904 for £185 for the Small Holdings Association in Newdigate, Surrey.

At the time there was much scepticism in the press as to the practicality of the exhibition and whether the cottages could be built in different circumstances for the same sum, or even if it was desirable to limit the quality of a building by such stringent means. Strachey, however, was adamant that if landowners could see that it was legally possible to build a cottage for £150, they would in fact do so — and so help to solve the rural housing shortage.

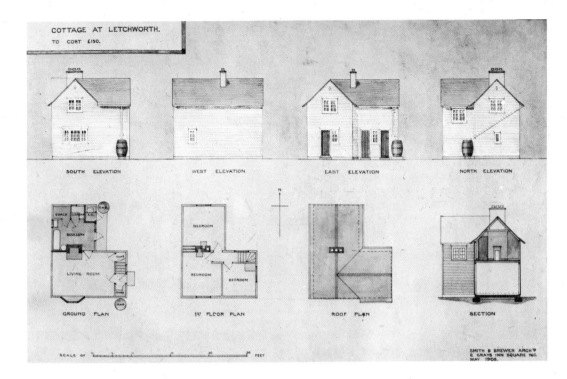

COTTAGE AT LETCHWORTH.
TO COST £150.

SOUTH ELEVATION   WEST ELEVATION   EAST ELEVATION   NORTH ELEVATION

GROUND PLAN   1ST FLOOR PLAN   ROOF PLAN   SECTION

SCALE OF   FEET

SMITH & BREWER ARCHTS
2 GRAYS INN SQUARE WC.
MAY 1905.

amalgamate all the aspects of the building industry in such a way as to encourage the proper utilization of skilled labour resources. His wife, Mrs Violet Penty, still lived at their home in Chiswick in 1964: to visit her was to step back in time. The floors were scrubbed white, the furniture designed in oak by Penty and Spooner, the chairs covered with a faded Morris Strawberry Thief.

It is ironic, however, that the Arts and Crafts tradition survived the longest in housing schemes for Rural District Councils (Fig. 134) and in the suburbs where half-timbered gables, lean-to porches, tile-hanging and hipped roofs were reproduced in their thousands by speculative builders in the inter-war period. Not all these suburban estates, however, were put up without architects. Sydney Castle, for example, was an architect who specialized in Neo-Tudor and who designed many houses and cottages in the Home Counties. From 1923-1928 he designed an estate of 300 houses, (the Barker Estate), at East Sheen, Surrey, most of them in an Arts and Crafts vernacular and of fine quality. We know of his work through his drawings as he did not try to promote himself.

The suburban buildings of the inter-war period have not as yet been fully researched and a fascinating field of exploration awaits anyone with a keen eye. They were built largely by architects who had been trained in the 1890s or early 1900s in architectural offices rather than in architectural schools, and who had absorbed through their pupilage the traditional ways of building.

Cost @ 4d per cub. ft.
£316 for Pair.

Pair of Labourers' Cottages. North Wales.

Block 'A'.

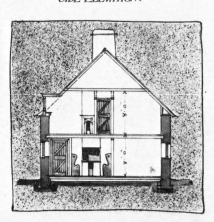

FRONT ELEVATION.

BACK ELEVATION.

SIDE ELEVATION.

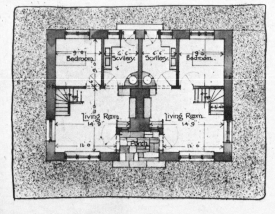

GROUND PLAN.

FIRST FLOOR PLAN.

SECTION.

Clough Williams Ellis
Architect.
Arundel House.
London. W.C.
December 1905.

128 Clough Williams-Ellis. Design for a pair of labourers' cottages in North Wales, to cost £316 for the pair, 1905. Pen and watercolour (400 x 520).

Clough Williams-Ellis became involved in the 'Cheap Cottage Movement' as early as 1905. He has followed the Letchworth pattern in providing a living room, scullery and two bedrooms, but his pair are to be built of good quality, durable materials — local stone, roughcast and slate. Clough later met his future father-in-law, St Loe Strachey when he won a competition organized by him for a £110 cottage which was built at Merrow Down in Surrey. He also built many cottages in Wales for the Festiniog District Slate Quarry Owners' Association, and made experimental designs for dwellings to be built of pisé (compressed earth). His book on *Cottage building in cob, pisé, chalk and clay*, which looked at ancient building methods, was published in 1919 at a time of acute housing shortage, and was reissued in 1947 to cope with similar circumstances.

129 Sir Edward Brantwood Maufe (1883-1974).
Design for Kelling Hall, Norfolk, for
H.W.A. Deterding, drawn by J.B. Scott, 1912.
Pen (335 x 540).

Kelling Hall is one of the 'last' large Arts and
Crafts houses. It was built on the coast and was
one of a number of Edwardian 'sun-trap' or
'butterfly' plan houses designed to make the
most of the sun. It followed the pattern of Prior's
Home Place, Holt, nearby, not only in its plan
but in a similar use of materials, gables and
hipped roof. Maufe had met the client,
H.W. Deterding, director general of Royal Dutch
Petroleum, at a dinner party and had gained the
commission on the strength of their conversation
that night; it was his first work of any size. The
house was built of grey knapped flint and brick,
with a grey tile roof, and was pronounced 'a
thoroughly vernacular work, never putting
undue strain on the King's architectural English'.
(Christopher Hussey in *Country Life*, LIII, 1923,
p. 349.) The brick, however, was mainly imported
from Holland. It is an expensive and superbly
crafted house — designed down to the smallest
detail. All the surviving drawings are at the RIBA
and include planting plans for all the trees, and
elaborately designed layouts for the herringbone
brickwork in the entrance forecourt.

130 Arthur Jessop Hardwick (1867-1948).
Design for The Thatched House, Gerrards Cross,
Middlesex, for T.D. McMeekin Esq., drawn by
Sydney Castle, *c.*1905. Print with coloured
washes (490 x 760).

Hardwick, who practised in Kingston-upon-
Thames, had a well-established practice in the
Thames Valley, and was well-known in both
England and Germany as an architect of rather
outré Arts and Crafts houses in the manner of
E. Turner Powell. The design was drawn by
Castle during the period he worked in Hardwick's
office, 1900-1908.

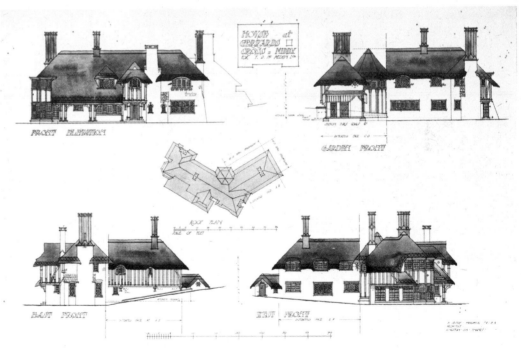

131 Sydney Ernest Castle (1883-1955) and Gerald Warren. Design for a 'Daily Mirror' cottage at Sheerwater Estate, Byfleet, Surrey, drawn by Sydney Castle, *c.*1912. Pen and watercolour (220 x 305).

Castle had studied drawing under Sydney Newcombe and Ernest Godman, to whom he owed much of his early knowledge of vernacular buildings, and in 1905 contributed illustrations to Godman's *Mediaeval Architecture in Essex*. In this Daily Mirror 'cottage' which was built in Byfleet, he has translated cottage vernacular into a quite substantial suburban house, but has retained the quality and traditional detail that is so characteristic of his work. Vernacular features, such as the gable and lean-to have been incorporated into the design; also visible are the ends of the roof joists, oak pegging and water-butt. Seen here, and in all his designs, are metal casement windows, based on the old Tudor lead casements, which Castle promoted for domestic use. In 1914 he wrote and illustrated a booklet, *Metal Casements, Old and New*, published by the International Casement Company, for whom he had produced pen drawings and historical information to assist in the promotion of metal windows and leaded lights. It is likely that Castle played some part in determining the standard size of metal windows adopted by manufacturers such as Crittall and Henry Hope.

132 Sydney Ernest Castle and Gerald Warren. Design for a house in Cavendish Road, St George's Hill, Weybridge, Surrey, drawn by Sydney Castle, 1914. Pen (245 x 310).

Castle's pen drawings, which are among the finest in the RIBA Drawings Collection, convey with great realism the different textures of natural building materials. He is able to differentiate brick from tile hanging, wood from plaster and by fine wavy lines to suggest a structure that has settled into place over the years. The drawing was exhibited at the Royal Academy in 1914; it pictured the secure life in a wealthy English suburb on the eve of the First World War. Castle was at his best designing in the Neo-Tudor style. He was an expert in Tudor domestic architecture and in 1928 wrote and illustrated *Domestic Gothic of the Tudor Period*.

133 Sydney Ernest Castle. Unexecuted design for a village war memorial, 1920. Pen (355 × 295).

At the end of the First World War the war memorial became *the* architectural set-piece. There was very little work on hand during the period 1919-1922 and the most common jobs available were often war memorials or private monuments in local churches. Many architects produced, as here, theoretical designs for exhibition or publication. Comparatively few memorials took the form of simple, rustic buildings. In the war cemeteries in France and Belgium the predominating style was an 'elemental' classicism, inspired by Lutyens, who together with Sir Reginald Blomfield and Sir Herbert Baker, were the three consultant architects to the Imperial War Graves Commission. Of the three only Baker favoured a more humble style, which he associated with the beauty of the churchyard and cloister, and he often introduced vernacular elements into his cemeteries.

LOOKING UP | LOOKING DOW'N

To our honoured dead.

A VILLAGE WAR MEMORIAL.

SYDNEY E CASTLE
ARCHITECT
28 DUKE ST. ST JAMES
SW1

1927 | The ERPINGHAM R·D·C HOUSING SCHEME at CLEY·NEXT·THE·SEA Norfolk | G.J. Skipper, F.R.I.B.A., M.T.P.I.

134 George John Skipper (1856-1948). Design for housing at Cley-next-the-Sea, Norfolk for the Erpingham Rural District Council, 1927. Print (265 x 700).

G.J. Skipper was the leading East Anglian architect at the turn of the century and designed such disparate buildings as the Norwich Union and the Royal Arcade in Norwich, the latter in a free Arts and Crafts style. In the 1920s he designed a number of local housing schemes for as many as ten Rural District Councils, experimenting with the cheaper kinds of building materials — clay-lump and flint — to meet the stringent financial climate of the time. These dwellings are of the 'parlour' type — that is they have a parlour *and* a living room, which was a more expensive prototype, and are pleasingly varied in their design and grouping.

135 Sydney Castle. Design for 'The Farthing' at Stowting, Kent for Mrs H.R. Payne, 1936-38. Pen (280 x 390).

Castle has used the familiar tile-hung elevation with hipped roof and half-timbering and herringbone brickwork in a traditional recess. The drawing shows his precise pen style and the clarity of his working details. Notice the way the lines cross one another as they meet (in the lower right hand corner, for example). This was a common technique during the Arts and Crafts period to avoid inexactness. The Farthing was Castle's last house.

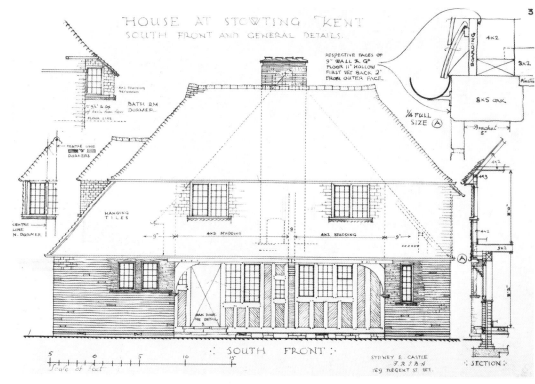

148

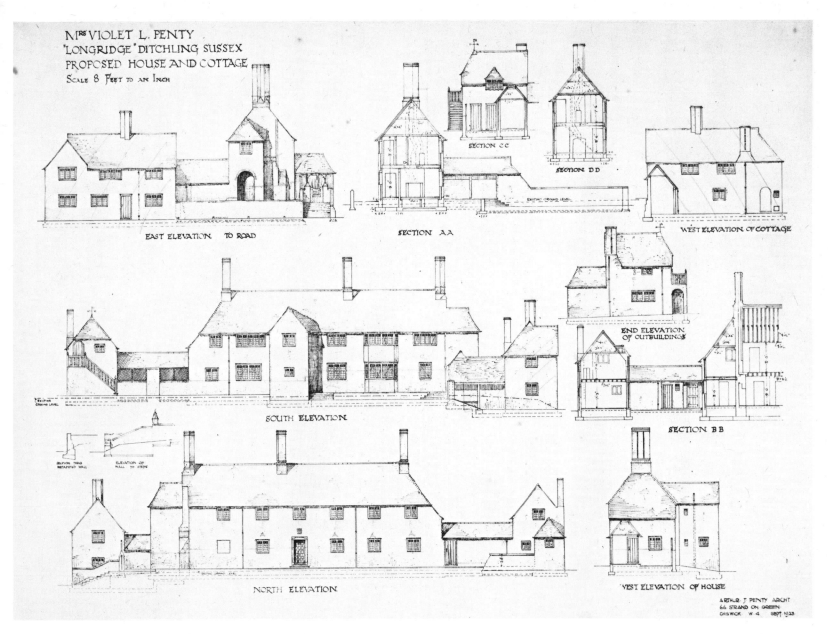

136 Arthur Joseph Penty (1875-1934). Design for 'Longridge' (Hillway), Ditchling, Sussex, for Mrs Violet L. Penty, 1923. Print with pencil additions and alterations (560 x 755).

A.J. Penty was a prominent member of the Art Workers' Guild in the 1920s and 30s and one of the architects who helped to extend the theories of the Arts and Crafts Movement well on into the twentieth century. He advocated a return to simple vernacular models as a source in building and set out his ideas in *The Elements of Domestic Design*, 1930, which is a plea for a return to the early rational ideas of the Movement. This design for his own house at Ditchling was used in his book to illustrate his theories. He suggested that the ideal source was the old English detached cottage with a single pitched roof. He recommended a simple parallelogram and that the architect should start his design with the roof plan. A house should be one room deep and the windows small and not necessarily set regularly.

The roofs should not have dormers (to avoid too many motifs) and features such as gable and hip should alternate sparingly on different elevations.

Select bibliography

General

Peter Davey *Arts and Crafts Architecture: The Search for Earthly Paradise*, London, 1980.

Alastair Service *Edwardian Architecture and its origins*, London, 1975.

Alastair Service *Edwardian Architecture: a Handbook to Building Design in Britain 1890-1914*, London, 1977.

Hermann Muthesius *Das Englische Haus*, (3 vols), Berlin, 1905. The first English edition is *The English House*, (1 vol) London, 1979.

T. Raffles Davison (ed) *The Arts Connected with Building*, London, 1909.

Lawrence Weaver *The 'Country Life' Book of Cottages*, London, 1913.

John Summerson *The Turn of the Century: Architecture in Britain around 1900*, Glasgow, 1976.

Gavin Stamp *The English House 1860-1914*, Catalogue of an exhibition, Building Centre, London, 1980.

Individual architects

Ernest Gimson: Mary Comino *Gimson and the Barnsleys*, London, 1981.

Robert Lorimer: Peter Savage *Lorimer and the Edinburgh Craft Designers*, Edinburgh, 1980.

Edwin Lutyens: Christopher Hussey *The Life of Sir Edwin Lutyens*, London, 1950.

Lutyens: the Work of the English Architect Sir Edwin Lutyens (1869-1944), catalogue of an exhibition, Hayward Gallery, London, 1981.

M.H. Baillie Scott: James D. Kornwolf *M.H. Baillie Scott and the Arts and Crafts Movement*, Baltimore and London, 1972.

R. Norman Shaw: Andrew Saint *Richard Norman Shaw*, London, 1976.

C.F.A. Voysey: J. Brandon-Jones and others *C.F.A. Voysey: Architect and Designer 1857-1941*, catalogue of an exhibition, Brighton Art Gallery and Museum, 1978.

David Gebhard *Charles F.A. Voysey, Architect*, Los Angeles, 1975.

Philip Webb: W.R. Lethaby *Philip Webb and His Work*, Oxford, 1935.

Gerald Callcott Horsley. Design for an iron hinge, made for the Quarto Imperial Club, II, 1892. Pen and wash (360 x 255).

Index of names

The pages on which subects are illustrated are given in italics.